Great Drawings from the
Collection of the Royal Institute of
British Architects

Great Drawings from the Collection of the Royal Institute of British Architects

Jill Lever and Margaret Richardson
Introduction by John Harris

RIZZOLI
NEW YORK

This exhibition is made possible by a generous grant from Henry J. Heinz II K.B.E. and Mrs. Heinz, the National Endowment for the Arts, the New York Council for the Humanities, and the New York State Council on the Arts. We also gratefully acknowledge the help of the Vincent Astor Foundation, Imperial Chemical Industries PLC, Manufacturers Hanover Trust, Marley Holdings (U.S.A.) Inc., Mr. and Mrs. J. Irwin Miller, the Samuel I. Newhouse Foundation, Pinewood Foundation, Reed Stenhouse Inc., Skidmore, Owings & Merrill and Thomas Tilling, Inc.

Published in the United States of America in 1983 by Rizzoli International Publications, Inc. 712 Fifth Avenue, New York, NY 10019

ISBN 0-8478-0481-X

Foreword

The Drawing Center presents with pride this exhibition that helps to celebrate its sixth anniversary. The Center is a nonprofit institution, founded in 1977, that seeks through exhibition and education to express the quality and diversity of drawing – unique works on paper – as a major art form. Each year the Center presents at least five exhibitions. Those of an historical nature such as *Great Drawings from the Collection of the Royal Institute of British Architects* complement our program of showing works by contemporary artists whose drawings are not yet represented by commercial galleries and are not ordinarily on view in New York. It is a particular pleasure to present these master drawings from the British Architectural Library of the Royal Institute of British Architects. The Drawings Collection is perhaps the most comprehensive body of architectural designs in the world. I want to thank John Harris, Curator of the Collection, Jill Lever and Margaret Richardson, Deputy Curators, and Jane Preger, Exhibitions Assistant, who have provided us with this exhibition and catalogue. Their graciousness and generosity have made this event a great pleasure. I also want to thank Conway Lloyd Morgan, the publisher, who has continually solved problems with grace and good cheer.

The organization of this exhibition was greatly facilitated by the constant support of the Directors of The Drawing Center.

Special thanks go to my colleagues William Irvine, Administrative Assistant, Marie Keller, Associate Curator, and Jane Fluegel, Director of Development. All of us thank the many work/study students and interns who have made our tasks easier and more pleasurable.

This exhibition will be circulated in the United States by The American Federation of Arts, New York. It is an honor to be associated with this distinguished organization. Since its founding in 1909 it has helped to broaden the knowledge and appreciation of the arts of the past and present, primarily through the circulation of exhibitions both here and abroad. Gratitude goes to Wilder Green, Director, and to Jane Tai and Susanna D'Alton of the American Federation of Arts.

Finally, I would like to thank the following people who have helped in innumerable ways:

James S. Ackerman
William Howard Adams
Mrs. Armand P. Bartos
Jo Blatti
Collins Bruce
Tom Freudenheim
Rosemarie Garipoli
Linda Gillies
Peter Gilmore
Henry J. Heinz II K.B.E. and Mrs. Heinz
Marife Hernandez
Spiro Kostof
Peter Laundy
Roy Leaf
David Lloyd-Jacob
Irvine R. MacManus, Jr.

Michael McCarthy
Mr. and Mrs. J. Irwin Miller
David Nathans
George Negroponte
Victoria Newhouse
Margot Paul
Christopher N. Robinson
Gilbert Robinson
Helen E. Searing
Martin E. Segal
Dr. N. Brian Smith
Damie Stillman
Harry Taylor
Marvin Trachtenberg
Brenda Trimarco
Massimo Vignelli
Bernard Walsh

Martha Beck Director, The Drawing Center

Contents

Introduction

From the Renaissance until modern times, architectural drawings have interested both collectors and connoisseurs. The architect, painter and biographer Giorgio Vasari (1511-74), for example, collected drawings by architects, but they took their place alongside his drawings by painters. As far as we know, neither architects nor collectors in the sixteenth century methodically compiled holdings of architectural drawings. This had to await the establishment of public museums and the foundation of professional institutions. In late seventeenth and early eighteenth century Europe although many academies retained architectural drawings in their archives – a notable example being the Accademia di San Luca in Rome –none of these architectural drawings were professionally organised or catalogued. This only occurred with the foundation of architectural museums. The first of these was the museum in London founded in 1833 by Sir John Soane (1753-1837), which was intended, according to its charter, to serve as an educational and public resource. It was, however, a static collection, comprising Soane's own working drawings and his collection of his contemporaries' work (notably drawings by Robert Adam.)

The foundation in 1834 of the Royal Institute of British Architects led to the creation of a library of architectural books and drawings, protected by charter and performing a complete museological function with displays and public lectures. The 'Soane' and the 'RIBA' can lay claim to be the first manifestations of the wish of architects to provide their successors with examples of the best or greatest in design.

Sir John Soane's collection, although distinguished and large, was not an exceptional case. Sir William Chambers had amassed a considerable number of architectural drawings, as had Robert Adam. The history of architects as collectors of architectural drawings began in England when Inigo Jones (1573-1652), the founder of classical architecture in England, and the Earl of Arundel acquired, from Vincenzo Scamozzi (1552-1616) in Venice in 1614, many of Andrea Palladio's architectural drawings together with all of Scamozzi's own. Scamozzi's have since been lost, but when all of Jones's designs for buildings and all those by his assistant, John Webb (1611-72) were added to the collection, its bulk and importance was great. It was a tremendous coup for William (1650-

1719) and John (1677-1726) Talman to have acquired most of the collection by about 1700. At its height, this collection was probably one of the greatest in Europe, contained in over 200 folio volumes 'four feet high'. In the rest of Europe there was only one comparable collection, in Sweden, formed by Nicodemus Tessin the elder (1615-81), the architect of the Drottningholm Palace in Stockholm, and his son, Nicodemus Tessin the younger (1654-1728). The fruits of this father and son partnership, which includes drawings by all the great architects working for Louis XIV of France as well as by garden designers such as Le Nôtre, is today one of the jewels in the crown of the Print Cabinet of the Nationalmuseum in Stockholm.

In England, through John Talman's intervention, the Palladio-Jones-Webb drawings were sold in 1720 and 1721 to Richard Boyle, 3rd Earl of Burlington (1694-1753). To these Burlington was to add Palladio's own drawings of Roman antiquity, bought by him, perhaps in Rome, in 1719. Thus in London in 1721 the original corpus of Palladio's drawings was re-united for the first time since the 1580s. The Burlington-Devonshire collection, as it became known, was given to the RIBA in 1894.

Inigo Jones, Talman, Burlington, Soane – these are among Britain's celebrated architect-collectors. As a professional institution the RIBA has received munificent gifts from its members, or from other collectors through the intervention of members. The magnificent Italian and French stage designs amassed by Sir John Drummond Stewart (died 1838) in the early nineteenth century were bequeathed to the Institute in 1838, probably through the persuasion of Earl de Grey, the Institute's first President, and an amateur architect of extraordinary ability. From 1834 on, the Institute has been fortunate that its members saw it as a right and proper place to either deposit or bequeath their drawings, and because of this the Institute's holdings of Victorian drawings are magisterial. In no other place is nineteenth century architectural design so well represented. Throughout Europe the nineteenth century was the great age for collecting drawings, and for selling them. The basis of the architectural drawings collection in the Kunstbibliothek in Berlin came from the French architect-collector Hippolyte Destailleur in 1879. Throughout the world architectural institutes acquired drawings, but never systematically or with any avowed policy.

The RIBA's Collection is also exceptional in that the Institution was able to attract bulk deposits of the work of a single architect or architect's office. Thus, J.B. Papworth, William Burn, Sir George Gilbert Scott, Michael Searles, C.F.A. Voysey, Detmar Blow, Sir Edwin Lutyens, Alfred Waterhouse, Ninian Comper, Ernö Goldfinger, are a few among the many architects whose large collections and archives, some in their entirety, are now preserved in the RIBA Drawing Collection.

This is a continuing process. Only in recent years have the great building firms founded in the nineteenth century been examined. As a consequence the RIBA holds, for example, the drawings of Dove Brothers. Such an archive is in itself a survey in miniature of architectural design between 1860 and 1920. Most of the items in such archives are what are known as working or contract drawings, very often torn, stained and rolled as a result of use 'on site', and very different from the fine draughtsmanship of earlier drawings.

This contrast is a symptom of the change of role of the Collection, from a treasury of 'old master' drawings to a national archive. This is also a concomitant of changes in attitudes to architectural history which have taken place since the 1950s.

What may be called the old master syndrome in collecting architectural drawings belongs to the realm of connoisseurship, and is evidence of the desire to select the finest examples of draughtsmanship by great artists. Great architects, however, by no means draw well. Whereas Inigo Jones was one of the finest draughtsmen in Europe, the drawings of Sir Christopher Wren (1632-1723), although pregnant with the power of architectural meaning, are crude by comparison.

In England standards of drafting were to improve following the foundation of the Royal Academy of Arts in 1768. Students were taught the techniques of drawing and colouring and a set of standards was established. The large practices of architects such as Sir William Chambers (1723-96) and Robert Adam (1728-92) themselves produced an office style in both drawing and handwriting. So in consequence the drawings of Thomas Hardwick (1752-1829) or Edward Stevens (c. 1744-1775) or James Gandon (1743-1823) all bear the signature of the style of Chambers, in whose office they received their training. When at the end of the eighteenth century Picturesque architecture came into fashion, in the work of architects such as John Nash (1752-1835), and it became almost obligatory to compose designs as pictures, architects had to add to the techniques of line and wash, skill in watercolour painting. As a result professional watercolour artists were often employed by architects to produce or render their designs and so by the 1830s it became impossible in many cases to distinguish between a topographical view and an architectural design. This is the case with watercolour designs by Edward Blore (1787-1879). This tendency was to increase throughout the nineteenth century, particularly with the rise in the number of architectural competitions, especially for municipal and public buildings, and by 1900 the perspectivist or perspective artist was much in demand.

This is not to say that architects abrogated the art of drawing, for to so many, good drawing came easily by virtue of their constant use of travel sketchbooks and the likes of C.R. Cockerell, Alfred Waterhouse, Edwin Alfred Rickards or Ernest George were superlative perspective artists in their own right. Generally the perspectivist was employed by the more successful architects in charge of the larger offices, and often the task was to prepare exhibits for the Royal Academy. It is often forgotten how important the Royal Academy exhibition, particularly the Architecture Room, was in the nineteenth and early twentieth centuries as a venue for

continued on page 25

I ROBERT SMYTHSON (3)

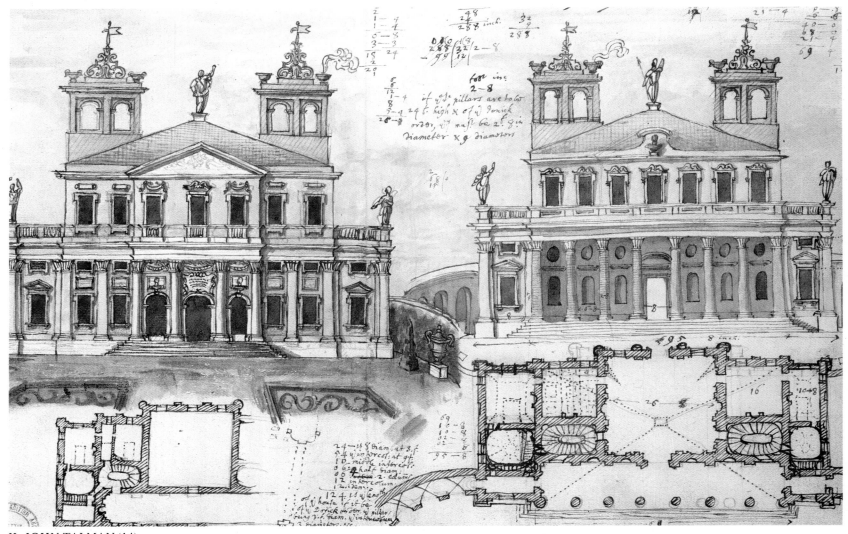

II JOHN TALMAN (14)

Section of York House November 1759

III SIR WILLIAM CHAMBERS (21)

IV JAMES STUART (23)

Perspective view ONSLOW HOUSE.

V GEORGE STEUART (25)

VI JOSEPH BONOMI (30)

VII ANON: ITIMAD-UD-DAULA (43)

VIII   JAMES WYATT (32)

IX R.L. ROUMIEU (50)

18

X J.L. PEARSON (55)

19

XI PHILIP BROWN (57)

XIII C.F.A. VOYSEY (68)

XIV ERNEST NEWTON (69)

XV GILES GILBERT SCOTT (75)

continued from page 8

attracting commissions. This importance is reflected in the fact that architectural presentation drawings tended to increase in size as the nineteenth century progressed.

Even at the height of the great age of the perspective the art was under attack from purists who believed, as did Ruskin and Morris, that a successful building process only needed minimal guidance between the imagination and the reality, a fallacy largely due to widespread misunderstanding of medieval cathedral design. It was in fact a short step from this belief to that of the Modern Movement where plan forms were minimal and a pure geometry reigned. The Minimal School stood in stark contrast to the concurrent Beaux-Arts manner. Looking through drawings of the 1920s and 1930s, this pure linearity where even colour was eschewed, except by the De Stijl movement and its followers, strikes a sterile note within the context of a synoptic drawings collection. The art of drawing for drawing's sake was debunked, and it is no coincidence that this same period reveals an absence of architects' travel sketchbooks. Even as late as the 1960s drawing and history were regarded as deleterious influences, and a well-known architectural historian who attended a London school of architecture was told that it was not necessary to draw to be an architect. In an age of upturned shoe-boxes perhaps this is true, and truer still in an age of computerised design. Designs were no longer studied as examples: it was rather buildings themselves or at least photographs of the buildings.

Between the two World Wars the architectural profession everywhere was uninterested in its own drawings, and only the practitioners in the classical tradition, those trained under the rules established by the Ecole des Beaux Arts in Paris, for example, were still interested in the practice of fine drawing and collected and cherished old drawings. Happily for the drawing cabinets and collections of the world, when these practitioners died or their offices closed, fine architectural drawings were released for acquisition. Some practices were, however, enabled to remain intact, and are immortalised in the names of institutions such as the Burnham Architectural Library of the Art Institute of Chicago, where, incidentally, resides a major portion of the library of Charles Percier of Percier and Fontaine. Most of the major architectural libraries and drawings collections in the United States were founded in the Beaux Arts period, such as the Cooper Hewitt Museum of Design, the Smithsonian Institution or the Avery Architectural Library of Columbia University. One must not forget, either, the national and state archives: the Library of Congress, the government architectural archives of Washington D.C., or the Historical Society of Pennsylvania. A

phenomenon emanating from the United States is the establishment of single office archives, such as the Mies van der Rohe archive with the Museum of Modern Art or the Louis Kahn Archive at the University of Pennsylvania.

Nevertheless, it is very noticeable that the boom in architectural drawings as a marketable commodity began in the 1950s and 1960s, decades that witnessed the death of a couple of dozen octogenarian architects, so releasing their collections of drawings and books onto the market. Reflecting back upon those halcyon decades, the boom was the prerogative of a happy band of collectors and museum curators, able to purchase masterpieces for minimal sums.

Today it is very different. Dealers and decorators vie with each other to buy the dwindling few great drawings, and pay huge sums for mediocre drawings by minor architects. Few dealers understand what they are buying and none have a proper grip on, or understanding of, architectural history or connoisseurship. They are unable to differentiate between a design, an office rendering, or a working or contract drawing, and the market is flooded with 'designs' for building types that are, in effect, theoretical student works. The antique and decorator's shops in Paris, for example, are full of expensively priced, flashy, drawings, most of which were hidden in shame by the student who eventually became an architect in his or her own right. None of these dealers is to blame. If they were trained in art or architectural history in one of our contemporary schools, they will never have heard of connoisseurship in architectural drawing. Architectural history is still taught by the blinkered myopic approach of dates, styles, architects, and, less often, physical examination of buildings. As a consequence, the literature about architectural drawings is derisory compared to that on old master drawings. Happily all this is changing. The late 1970s witnessed a burgeoning of exhibitions of architectural drawings and many of the leaders of Post-Modern architecture are masters in the art of drawing. The more architectural drawings exhibitions there are the better, for only by exposure to architectural drawings will appreciation and understanding be achieved. The Drawing Center in New York has a reputation as a venue for exhibitions of drawings in that part of the city called Soho, a hive of activity by smaller galleries of art and photography. To introduce a selection of the best architectural drawings from the Royal Institute of British Architects to this part of downtown New York should not be seen as a lesser alternative to Fifth Avenue, but as a widening of the parameters of interest in such drawings. And that is surely the best of reasons.

John Harris, London, March 1983

Sources and further reading

A brief bibliography (*Lit.*) is given with the entry for each drawing. Further information on the drawings, buildings and architects discussed can be found in the following;-

Catalogue of the Drawings Collection of the R.I.B.A. (Farnborough and Amersham, 1969-83) General editor: Jill Lever. Volumes available; A,B, C-F, G-K, L-N, O-R, S, T-Z (*in preparation*), Colen Campbell, Jacques Gentilhâtre, Inigo Jones & John Webb, Edwin Lutyens, J.B. Papworth, Pugin Family, Scott Family, Alfred Stevens, Antonio Visentini, C.F.A. Voysey, Wyatt Family.

RIBA Drawings Series (London and New York 1981-3) Volumes available: The Palladians (John Harris), The Great Perspectivists (Gavin Stamp), Architects' Designs for Furniture (Jill Lever), Architects of the Arts and Crafts Movement (Margaret Richardson), The Thirties (David Dean).

The Buildings of England (Harmondsworth, 1957 to date) N. Pevsner & others. 50 volumes.

Colvin, H. *A Biographical Dictionary of British Architects 1600 – 1840* (2nd ed. London, 1978).

Illustrations

The drawings reproduced here are all from the Drawings Collection of the R.I.B.A., except nos. 80, 81 and 82, which are lent by the architects.

The sizes of drawings are given in millimetres and inches: height precedes width.

Late Medieval and after

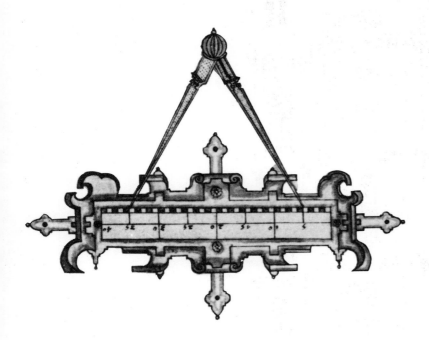

Dividers and scale, a detail taken from a drawing by Robert Smythson, c. 1609.

The first group of drawings shown here have in common that they are early examples of architectural designs and were made by architects who received their initial training as stonemasons. The examples of architecture, from England, France and northern Italy range in date from the late fifteenth century to the 1620s.

The earliest of the designs, for a tower with turrets but also with large windows, demonstrates the new political stability of Tudor England as well as the romantic taste of its Court. The design for a chantry chapel was among the last of such works, for the social changes made by the Reformation of Henry VIII brought a halt to ecclesiastical building in England. It marks too, the final phase of medieval Gothic architecture while the squareness, symmetry and great windows of the tower design were to become the hallmarks of Elizabethan domestic architecure. They are found in Robert Smythson's design, of about 1590, for a country house, allied to a gable probably derived from a Dutch pattern book and an arcaded loggia entrance with Doric pilasters that is Italianate. Though John Smythson's design for a room in Bolsover Castle shows the influence of imported ideas, Elizabethan architecture was largely untouched by the Renaissance in continental Europe. Despite some occasional solecisms in the matter of decorative details, the novelty, daring and unity of the best examples are unparallelled elsewhere.

In France, Italian Renaissance influence was apparent by the first years of the sixteenth century and from 1546, with the rebuilding of the Louvre, a national Renaissance style developed. The overcrowded facade, pavilion roof and fantastical details of Gentilhâtre's design for a house reveal an unmistakable French Mannerism, derived from du Cerceau the Elder and used here in a *retardataire* way by a provincial architect.

The Renaissance came later to Genoa than to other Italian cities and the Palazzo del Signor Antonio Doria represents an early stage in the development of a distinctive Genoese style that favoured a Mannerist freedom combined with the use of local traditions. The use here of an arcuated cornice found in Lombardy is unique but the ornate ornament (some of it painted) and the decorative emphasis on the entrance are typically Genoese.

1 English late 15th century master
Design for a tower with turrets.
Perspective
Sepia pen & coloured washes on vellum
(19⅛ × 7⅞) (485 × 200)
Provenance:?; Robert Smythson (1535-1614);
John Smythson (died 1634); Huntingdon
Smythson (died 1648); John Smythson the
Younger (1640-1777); ?; sold by the 5th Lord
Byron at Newstead Abbey, Nottinghamshire,
June 1778, lot 344; there bought by the Rev
D'Ewes Coke of Broke-hill Hall, Derbyshire; by
descent to Mrs S. Coke of Broke-hill Hall from
whom the drawing with others was purchased by
the RIBA in 1927

English architectural drawings of the medieval
period are exceedingly rare and this design for a
four-storey tower with turrets is the earliest in the
RIBA Drawings Collection. Details such as the
rectangular frame to each of the openings and
the general lack of cusping tend to suggest a date
of around 1500.

Splendid enough to have been intended for a
royal palace or castle, the naively drawn
perspective may have come from the Office of
the King's Works, the department of government
that maintained and built royal residences. If
that were the case then the design (more a
presentation drawing than a working drawing)
would have been made for Henry VII who
reigned 1485-1509. The first of the Tudor
monarchs, he restored order within the kingdom
and thus made castles redundant. However, the
essential contradiction of a tower with all the
defensive paraphernalia of turrets, crenellations
and arrow loops, allied to very large and
unmilitary windows is explained by the romantic
love of chivalry of the Tudor court. If it was built,
the tower has not survived.

Lit: M. Girouard, 'The Three Gothic Drawings in
the Smythson Collection', *RIBA Journal*, 3rd
series, LXIV, 1956, pp.35-6

See back cover

2 English 16th century master, perhaps Thomas
Berty (c. 1485-1555)
Design for one bay of Bishop Fox's chantry
chapel, Winchester Cathedral, Hampshire
Elevation
Sepia pen (37½ × 11¾) (955 × 295)
Provenance: as given for no. 1

Chantry chapels were built within a church or
cathedral so that masses could be sung there for
the soul of their founder. In 1547 such chapels
were suppressed in the Reformation Movement
of Tudor England. Thus Richard Fox, Bishop of
Winchester, who died in 1528, received only a
limited benefit from the building of his chantry
chapel in the south aisle of Winchester
Cathedral.

The design for one of the four bays, shown
here, was drawn in elevation except for the
niches which were drawn in perspective. As built,
the chantry varies in some details as well as in
proportion from the drawing. There are, for
instance, eight niches not the six shown here and
this is because the height of the chantry chapel is
3½ times its width rather than the 2½ times
suggested in this design.

The architect for Bishop Fox's chantry
(completed some years before the Bishop's
death) may have been Thomas Berty whose work
at Winchester Cathedral from about 1517 was
done during the period of transition from Gothic
to Tudor-Renaissance. So that while Berty's
design (if it is his) for the chapel is in an
accomplished late Perpendicular style, it has
nevertheless a Renaissance feeling about it.

Another of his works in the same building
does make use of Italian Renaissance decoration.

Lit: as for no. 1

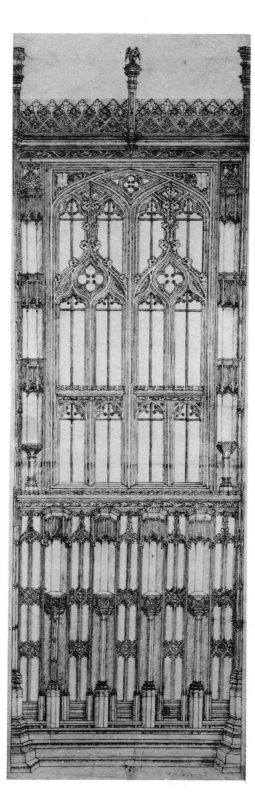

3 Robert Smythson (*c.* 1535-1614)
Design for a country house, *c.* 1590
Elevation of the entrance front.
Sepia pen & coloured washes (12¾ × 18½)
(325 × 470)
Provenance: Robert Smythson; and subsequently
as given for no. 1

Robert Smythson, a leading mason-trained
architect of the time of Elizabeth I, designed a
number of country houses in the Midlands and
North of England. Of these, Longleat House in
Wiltshire, Wollaton Hall and Worksop Manor in
Nottinghamshire and Hardwick Hall in
Derbyshire are the most important. They
establish Smythson as an important and
innovative designer and one of the creators of the
Elizabethan style.

The design for an unidentified country house
shown here has the stepped plan and the towers
of Hardwick Hall, *c.* 1590, while the central gable
is a simplified version of those at Wollaton Hall
designed for Sir Francis Willoughby in 1580. The
main lines of the drawing were incised by
Smythson with a blank stylus before using a well-
sharpened quill pen and ink. For the rendering
of the glass to the windows he tried hatching and
cross-hatching for what must have been a
presentation drawing for an important patron.
The balustrade to the stair reveals Smythson's
unsophisticated draughtsmanship.

Smythson died in 1614 and his monument in
Wollaton church (probably designed by his son,
John) reads: 'Here lyeth ye body of Mr Robert
Smythson, gent, Architect & Survayor unto the
most worthy house of Wollaton with diverse
others of great account...'. Was he the first man
in England to have 'Architect' inscribed on his
tombstone?

Lit: M. Girouard, 'The Smythson Collection of
the Royal Institute of British Architects',
Architectural History, V, 1962; pp. 42, 109;
M. Girouard, *Robert Smythson and the Architecture of the
Elizabethan Era*, London, 1966, p.122, fig.72

see Plate I

4 John Smythson (died 1634)
Design for a room in the Little Castle, Bolsover
Castle, Derbyshire, c. 1625
Interior perspective & plan
Sepia pen & wash with some pencil inscriptions
(9 × 4¾) (230 × 120)
Provenance: John Smythson; and subsequently
as given for no.1

John Smythson worked on the Little Castle at
Bolsover Castle from 1612 to the mid 1620s and
the design for a room, shown here, must have
been made before or around 1625. Its marble-
vaulted ceiling, painted decoration, wall
hangings under a cornice, corner chimneypiece
and shuttered *French Windows* with a *Pergulae* (or
balcony) outside, indicate a concern with the
architectural unity of a room as well as an
awareness of new fashions in architectural
elements. The hooded chimneypiece, for
example, is among the earliest known example
of this kind in England. Smythson's taste for
novelty was greatly stimulated by a visit he made
to London in 1618-19. There he drew details of
some of Inigo Jones's recently completed works
including windows, doors and balconies in the
'Italyan' fashion which Smythson was then to add
to his own design vocabulary.

As a drawing, John Smythson's design is of
great interest for it is the earliest English example
(in the RIBA Drawings Collection) of an interior
perspective. But the sophistication of that idea is
modified by the naive use of cut-out flaps to
indicate window shutters.

The room, known as the Elysium room, exists
still, though the marble vault is now in another
room on the same floor of the Little Castle,
where it was presumably moved at a later date.

Lit: M. Girouard, 'The Smythson Collection of
the Royal Institute of British Architects',
Architectural History, V, 1962, pp.48, 127;
M. Girouard, *Robert Smythson and the Architecture of the
Elizabethan Era*, London, 1966, pp. 186-7;
J. Lever, *Architects' Designs for Furniture*, London,
1982, pp.12, 13

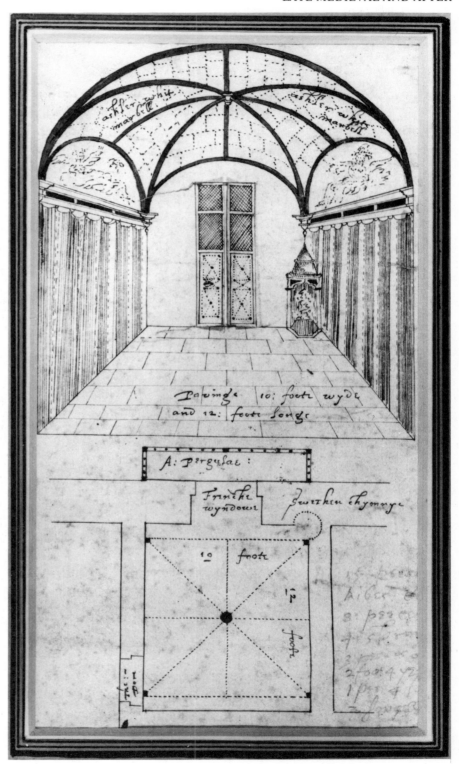

5 Jacques Gentilhâtre (born 1578)
Design for a house
Elevation of the principal front, to a scale of
approx. 1/10 inch to 1 *pied*
Bistre pen with blue, red & green washes on f. 25
recto of an album of 294 leaves
(9⅞ × 6¾) (250 × 170)
Provenance: ?: purchased in 1927 from a Mr
R. Watts.

A mason-trained architect, Jacques Gentilhâtre
was born at Sainte–Menehoul in north-eastern
France, *le 6 aovt 1578*. That fact is recorded on
the last page of his album of drawings (dated
from 1600 to 1623) of architecture, sculpture and
decoration. Had the album not survived,
Gentilhâtre would have been for us yet another
of 'the authors of innumerable, anonymous,
charming French provincial buildings of the first
half of the seventeenth century'.

The importance of Gentilhâtre's album lies not
in the quality of his designs nor of the buildings
by other architects that he records, for when he
drew them they were of a style that was already
old-fashioned. Conservative in his tastes and
undistinguished as a draughtsman, nevertheless
Gentilhâtre offers an insight on a difficult and
obscure period of French architecture.

The design shown here for an unidentified
house of five bays and two storeys with a high-
pitched roof, fanciful dormer windows and
heavily rusticated walls is in the decorative
Mannerist style of the late 16th century derived
from the engraved designs of Jacques Androuet
du Cerceau the Elder (*c.* 1520-1584).

Lit: R. Coope, *Jacques Gentilhâtre, Catalogue of the
Drawings Collection of the Royal Institute of British
Architects*, Farnborough, 1972, pp. 7-9, 13

6 *Made for* Sir Peter Paul Rubens (1577-1640)
Elevation of the principal front of the Palazzo
del Signor Antonio Doria, Acquasole, Genoa
drawn by an unidentified artist, to a scale of
0.077 in to 1 *palmo*
Pen, bistre pen & wash (11⅝ × 15⅝) (295 × 390)
Provenance: ? ; Sir Thomas Francklyn Bt (died
1728); ?; M. H. Marvey; sold at Sotheby's, 1906;
there bought by Welbore St Claire Baddeley who
in 1919 presented the bound volume of 122
drawings to the RIBA (17 of the original 137
drawings are lacking)

This is one of the original drawings made under
the direction of Peter Paul Rubens, for Plate XIV,
'Palazzi Moderni' in *Palazzi di Genova*, a record of

Facciata del Palazzo del Sig.ᵉ Antonio marchese di S.to Steffano.   *Doria Marchese de S Steffano —*

thirty-one palaces and villas and four churches, in or near Genoa in northern Italy. The drawings were made around 1607 and published from 1622 by Rubens. A leading artist of his generation, Rubens was also a diplomat in the service of the Spanish government and it is perhaps this that explains his publishing enterprise. Genoa was then a flourishing city state whose merchant-bankers funded the Spaniards in their expanding enterprises. It would have been rather flattering to the Genoese

to have their houses published as architectural exemplars. And, indeed Italian palazzo architecture was to become extremely influential in northern Europe. Rubens, when he settled in Antwerp in 1608, built himself a palace in the Italian style. The great esteem that Rubens enjoyed in England, ensured a wide readership for *Palazzi di Genova* and the book had some influence in the development of Artisan Mannerism, the mid-17th century popular style of architecture that succeeded Jacobean.

The architect of the palazzo built for Antonio Doria, *c.* 1542 is not known though attributions have been made to Bernardino Cantone da Cabio and to Caranchetto. Now the Palazzo della Prefettura (in the largo Lanfranco1) the building has been much altered over the years but the fine entrance with its coupled columns remains much as it was when drawn for Rubens.

33

Palladio and Palladianism

Palladio is the only architect to have given his name to an architectural style that has scarcely been out of use since its invention. Palladio's influence has been felt through his buildings, his books – in particular, the *Quattro Libri dell' Architettura* – and his drawings. Howard Burns, a modern scholar of Palladio, has written that 'Palladio provides the classic example of how an architectural system, providing for demanding functional, structural and aesthetic requirements can be developed, in theory and practice, without being over-rigid, or resulting in too uniform or boring buildings. He also shows how a basic adherence to method and system need not impede, and can facilitate the creation of totally new solutions.'

Aside from what was suggested by the brief, the site and the structural and aesthetic possibilities of stuccoed brick, stone and timber, Palladio's authorities were Nature – 'Nature, mother and mistress of all good things' – and the ideas on Roman architecture that he derived from Vitruvius's treatise and from his own researches. He was indebted also to other Italian architects of the time, such as Sebastiano Serlio. Palladio is best known as a designer of villas that housed not only the owner but also his steward, labourers and farm animals in a complex that included farmyards and farm buildings, gardens and orchards. The Villa Rotonda, too near to Vicenza to have these agricultural appendages, is the most famous of Palladio's villas. It has, on all four elevations, the temple-front portico that is perhaps the most influential of Palladio's contributions to domestic architecture.

Palladio's *Quattro Libri* was first published, in Venice, in 1570 and other editions soon followed. Inigo Jones took with him on his second trip to Italy (1613-14) a copy of the 1601 edition and made notes on the buildings as he visited them. While in Venice, by a stroke of good fortune that helped to change the course of English architecture, Jones was able to buy virtually all of Palladio's surviving design drawings from either Palladio's son, Silla or else Palladio's disciple, Vincenzo Scamozzi, an architect much respected by Jones.

The result of Inigo Jones's visit to Italy became evident, for example, in his designs for the Queen's House at Greenwich (1616-18 and 1629-35), the Prince's Lodging at Newmarket and the Banqueting House in Whitehall, London (1619-22). The Queen's House was the first strictly classical building in England, the Prince's Lodging became the source for English country houses of the later seventeenth century, and the Banqueting House perfectly expressed his dictum that architecture should be 'solid, proportionate to the rules, masculine and unaffected'.

Detail of a capital from the Temple of Hadrian, Rome, measured and drawn by Andrea Palladio in the early 1550s.

8

7 Andrea Palladio (1508-1580)
Half-elevation of the facade and half-section
through the projected cortile of the Palazzo da
Porto Festa, Vicenza, to a scale of 3/16 inch to
1 Vicentine foot
Pen & wash over incised lines (11½ × 14¾)
(290 × 375)
Provenance: ? Silla, son of Palladio; 1613-15,
Inigo Jones (1573-1652); Jones's assistant, John
Webb (1611-1672); William, son of John Webb,
who died prematurely; c. 1681, John Oliver (c.
1616-1701); William Talman (1650-1719); John,
son of William Talman (1677-1726); 1721, Lord
Burlington (1694-1753); Charlotte, daughter of
Lord Burlington and wife of the 4th Duke of
Devonshire; in 1894 presented to the RIBA by
the 8th Duke of Devonshire. For a fuller account
see Volume *B* of the *Catalogue of the Drawings
Collection of the Royal Institute of British Architects*,
Farnborough, 1972, p.119

These two preparatory drawings (there are two
sheets joined) for pages 9 and 10 of Book II of
Quattro Libri dell'Architectura show (on the left) the
facade of the Palazzo da Porto Festa and (on the
right) an unexecuted design for a cortile or
courtyard, with giant composite columns.
    About 1549, Palladio designed for Guiseppe

Porto a palazzo of seven bays with a piano nobile
articulated by an order above a rusticated
ground floor. That is, the standard palazzo
scheme based on Bramante's House of Raphael.
In some details, this drawing differs from both
the published plate and the executed building.
For instance, in the building (it survives still), the
voussoirs to the ground floor windows number
five and are arranged fan-wise. In plate 9 of the
Quattro Libri there are also five voussoirs but the
centre three are of an equal height. In the
drawing shown here, there are four voussoirs all
of the same height. It is interesting to see
Palladio on each occasion re-inventing the
solution to a detail that must have had particular
interest for him.
    When preparing the drawings for the *Quattro
Libri* (published 1570) Palladio made a theoretical
proposal for a twin to the Palazzo Porto joined
by a cortile at courtyard, the half-section of
which is shown here.

Lit: H. Burns, L. Fairbairn & B. Boucher, *Andrea
Palladio, The Portico and the Farmyard*, catalogue of
an exhibition, London, 1975, pp. 232-4; D.
Lewis, *The Drawings of Andrea Palladio*, catalogue of
an exhibition, Washington, 1981, pp. 210-11

8 Andrea Palladio (1508-1580)
Alternative designs for the scene front at the
Teatro Olimpico, Vicenza, 1580
Half-elevation drawn by Marc'Antonio Palladio,
nephew of Andrea Palladio, to a scale of approx.
¼ inch to 1 Vincentine foot
Pen & wash (16½ × 35¼) (420 × 895)
Provenance: as given for no. 7

The design of the Teatro Olimpico was based
upon Palladio's ideas about the appearance of
ancient Roman theatres with their fixed scenes
that had illusionistic receding 'streets' painted in
the openings.
    Of the alternative half-elevations for the fixed
scene front to the stage, it is the right-hand one
that is closest to the design as built. The drawing
seems to have been intended as a draft for the
sculptural programme. For this reason, no
doubt, Palladio delegated the making of it to his
nephew Marc'Antonio who as a sculptor was
better able to draw the proposed statues. These
were representations of such members of the
Accademica Olimpico as could afford to pay for
his own Roman-clad, heroically-posed portrait.
    The theatre, built of wood and plaster, its
exterior left to chance and hidden by nearby
buildings, was completed, four years after

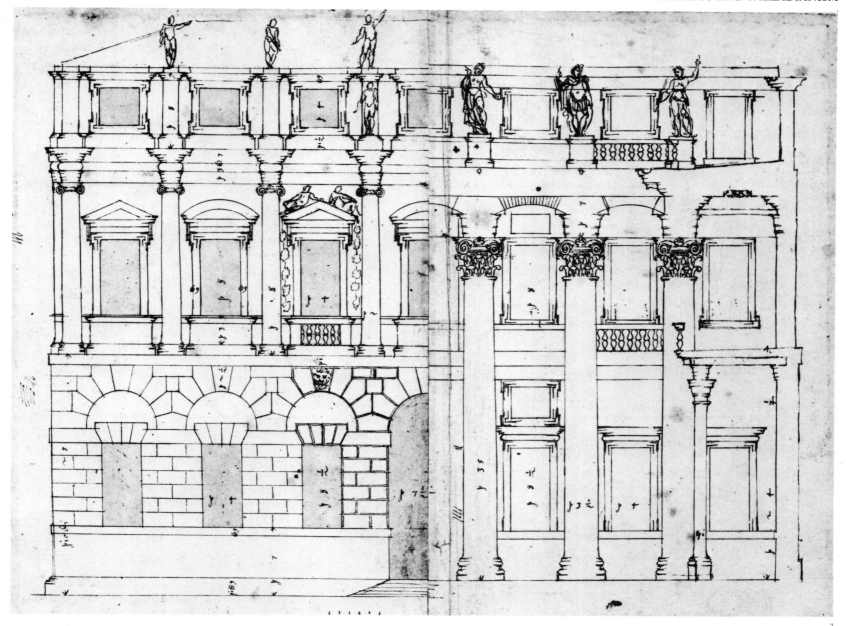

7

Palladio's death in 1584. Astonishingly, it survives and is still used for its original purpose.

Lit: J. S. Ackerman, *Palladio*, Harmondsworth, 1966, pp. 178-82; H. Burns, L. Fairbairn & B. Boucher, *Andrea Palladio, The Portico and the Farmyard*, catalogue of an exhibition, London, 1975, pp. 42-7; D. Lewis, *The Drawings of Andrea Palladio*, catalogue of an exhibition, Washington, 1981, pp. 210-11

9 Inigo Jones (1573-1652)
Alternative designs for the Prince's Lodging,
Newmarket Palace, Cambridgeshire, c. 1619
Elevations
Pen & wash (7⅞ × 11 & 7½ × 10⅞)
(195 × 280 & 190 × 275)
Provenance: John Webb (1611-72) and
subsequently as given for no. 7

In 1615 Inigo Jones was appointed Surveyor-
General of the King's Office of Works and thus
became responsible for the design of any new
buildings required by James I. When a 'lodging'
that is, separate quarters, was needed for

Charles, Prince of Wales, at the royal hunting
seat at Newmarket, the Surveyor-General offered
alternative proposals. Of these, the design with
columns is strongly Palladian and its source must
lie in Palladio's design for a town house for the
Capra family illustrated in his *Quattro Libri*, II,
plate 14. Jones has, though, expanded Palladio's
five-bay front to seven bays and added rusticated
detail derived from Serlio. As John Summerson
has explained, the elevation is organised on a
module derived from the width of all the
windows except for the centre window. Allowing
a value of four feet to the module this suggests a
total width of 68 feet. The astylar design is of

about the same width and, except for the
columns, has much the same features as the
other design. However, the proportions are quite
different and the roof with its large pedimented
dormer windows has become a much stronger
element. The freedom and inventiveness of the
astylar design marks Jones's growing
independence of Palladian sources.

A reduced version of the design without
columns seems to have been built. Like the
Prince for whom it was designed and who
became king in 1625 the 'lodging' had a short
life. By about 1650, with most of the rest of
Newmarket Palace, it was demolished by Colonel

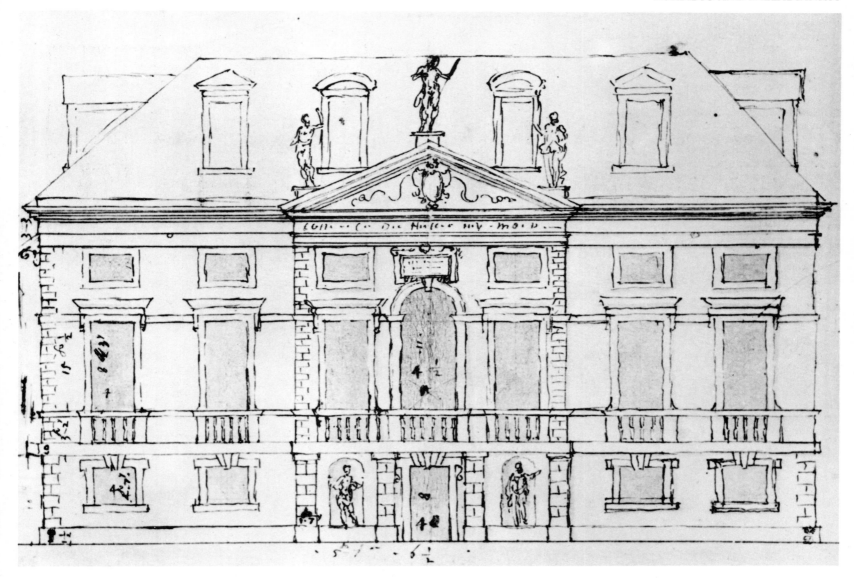

John Okey, one of the men who in 1649 signed
the warrant of execution for Charles I.

Lit: J. Summerson, *Inigo Jones*, Harmondsworth,
1966, pp. 58-60; J. Harris, *Inigo Jones & John
Webb, Catalogue of the Drawings Collection of the Royal
Institute of British Architects*, Farnborough, 1972, p.
16; *The King's Arcadia: Inigo Jones and the Stuart
Court*, catalogue of an exhibition, London, 1973,
pp. 112-117

10 Inigo Jones (1573-1652)
Design for the re-fronting of St Paul's Cathedral,
City of London
West elevation
Pen, wash & pencil (18⅛ × 19¾) (460 × 500)
Provenance: as given for no. 9

By 1608 the medieval cathedral of St Paul's
was in a very decrepit state and proposals were
made for its restoraton. Lack of funds meant that
work did not begin until 1633 and in the years
between, Jones made this design for a new west
front. Jones's built design (from the evidence of
the drawing published in William Kent, *Designs of
Inigo Jones*, 1727) was radically different from the
earlier scheme which has been described by John
Summerson as 'backcloth architecture'.
Rusticated masonry is used with little
understanding and there is a slightly unscholarly
use of motifs derived from Serlio and others. It is
likely that the design shown here was made in
about 1608, the year that marks the beginning of
Jones's transformation from 'picture-maker' to
the first English architect of genius.

The Great Fire of London of 1666 reduced old
St Paul's to a shell and after attempts to salvage at
least part of it proved hopeless, Sir Christopher
Wren was appointed to design a new St Paul's.

Lit: J. Summerson, *Inigo Jones*, Harmondsworth,
1966, pp. 28, 96-106; J. Harris, *Inigo Jones & John
Webb, Catalogue of the Drawings Collection of the Royal
Institute of British Architects*, Farnborough, 1972, p.16

The Baroque in England

The *Penguin Dictionary of Architecture*'s definition of Baroque as 'characterised by exuberant decoration, expansive, curvaceous forms, a sense of mass, a delight in large-scale and sweeping vistas and a preference for spatially complex compositions' makes it clear that English Baroque was never as whole-hearted as that of Italy (where it began), Spain, S. Germany or Austria, countries in which Baroque expressed the triumph of Catholicism after the traumas of the Reformation as well as the power of absolute monarchy. Puritan England, with its northerly climate and impoverished sovereigns watched by a Parliament jealous of its rights, was scarcely likely to achieve so joyfully spontaneous a Baroque style as its European neighbours. But in 1663, John Webb (1611-1672) designed the King Charles Building at Greenwich in a style that in its bold and simple massing and use of rustication and the giant order, prophesied the arrival of Baroque in England. Two years later, Christopher Wren visited Paris and met Bernini, and thus another step was taken in the development of an alternative to both the Classical Palladian architecture of Inigo Jones and his followers and the more informal brick architecture of Artisan Mannerism.

Sir Christopher Wren was the father of an English Baroque that since it was tempered by classical elements should more exactly be termed Baroque Classicism. Wren's Naval Hospital at Greenwich (from 1694) is the most integrated and grandest of his Baroque works even though it fell short of his original plan. Nicholas Hawksmoor (*c.* 1661-1736), Sir John Vanbrugh (1664-1726) and, to a lesser extent, Thomas Archer (*c.* 1668-1743) were Wren's successors. Vanbrugh and Hawksmoor worked together on the design of Blenheim Palace. Built for the Duke of Marlborough, victor of the Battle of Blenheim (1704) and more a national monument than a home, it represents the culmination of English Baroque. Appropriately, Sir James Thornhill, England's leading decorative painter in the Baroque manner, was to work both at Blenheim and Greenwich.

Early, though ephemeral, examples of the use of Baroque in English architecture were Sir Balthazar Gerbier's designs for temporary triumphal arches for the Coronation of Charles II, 1661. John Talman's Roman-Baroque design for a Trianon for King William came to nothing as did most building projects for British monarchs at that time. Our section on the Baroque in England ends with an acknowledgment to Italy – the source of Baroque. The Galli Bibiena design for a stage set, 1728, expresses by its sumptous illusionism, the high point of Baroque architecture.

Plans, elevation and section of the church of St Mary-le-Bow, Cheapside in the City of London, designed by Sir Christopher Wren. The steeple was completed in 1680 and Colen Campbell drew these details for publication in *Vitruvius Britannicus*, 1715-25.

11 Sir Balthazar Gerbier (1592-1663) and Peter Mills (1598-1670)
Design for a triumphal arch for the Coronation of Charles II, 1661, erected in Fleet Street, near Whitefriars in the City of London
Elevation, to a scale of approx. 1¾ inches to 10 feet
Sepia pen & grey wash (19⅝ × 10¼) (500 × 260)
Provenance: ?; Lord Burlington (1694-1753); Charlotte, daughter of Lord Burlington and wife of 4th Duke of Devonshire; in 1894 presented to the RIBA by the 8th Duke of Devonshire

Gerbier was a courtier, diplomat, painter of miniatures, occasional architect and much else besides. Mills, who began as a bricklayer and tiler, became an architect and surveyor, designing Thorpe Hall near Peterborough (1653-4), a major monument of Artisan Mannerism. Despite Mills's connections with Oliver Cromwell's Parliamentary party, his anti-Royalist sympathies did not prevent his employment as designer of the triumphal arches erected to celebrate the Coronation of Charles II. They were designed with 'another Person, who desired to have his name conceal'd'. Almost certainly this was Sir Balthazar Gerbier who despite the knighthood conferred on him by Charles I in 1638 showed himself during the Interrregnum as only too anxious, in his architectural capacity, to serve the Puritans and was, not unnaturally, banned from Court after the Restoraton. Hence the anonymity of his contribution.

The design for a 100 foot high triumphal arch, shown here, represents the 'Garden of Plenty'. Other designs were for the 'Return of the Monarchy', 'Loyalty Restored' and 'Temple of Concord'. They were erected by the City of London 'participating [in] the greatest share of the inexpressible Happiness, which these Kingdoms have received by the glorious Restoration of our Sovereign to His Throne'. In the description, published by John Ogilby, of *The Entertainment of His Most Excellent Majestie Charles II in His Passage Through the City of London for His Coronation*, 1662, Ogilby wrote that on the balconies beneath the twin arches stood twelve singers, six trumpeters and three drummers while on a stage before the arch, a 'woman representing Plenty read a rhyming address of homage to the King'.

The florid Baroque style of the triumphal arches resembles those designed by Rubens for the entry of Cardinal Infante Ferdinand into Antwerp in 1635 and published as *Pompa Introitus*, Antwerp, 1642. Gerbier, born and educated in Holland, knew and admired Rubens's work and his co-authorship of the triumphal arch seems thus confirmed.

12 Sir Christopher Wren (1632-1723)
Design for the dome over the Painted Hall of the
Royal Hospital, Greenwich, London, 1702
Plan, half-elevation and half-section drawn by
Nicholas Hawksmoor (c. 1661-1736), to a scale of
4 inches to 10 feet
Sepia pen & grey wash (27 × 18½) (685 × 470)
Provenance: ?; presented to the RIBA by
T. L. Donaldson, in 1843

Wren, a distinguished astronomer, designed his
first building, Pembroke College Chapel,
Cambridge, in 1663 when he was thirty-one.
This interest in architecture as an intellectual
diversion developed into a career that included
the design of the new cathedral of St Paul's, over
fifty churches, major works at Oxford and
Cambridge and the great hospitals at Chelsea
and Greenwich. His appointment as Surveyor
General of the King's Works in March 1668/9
gave Wren responsibility for all the royal
buildings and in 1694 when it was decided to
complete the partly built Palace at Greenwich,
Wren took charge. His Clerk of Works was
Nicholas Hawksmoor who had assisted him
almost from boyhood.

Wren's final overall design for the Naval
Hospital consisted of a succession of courtyards
with a Chapel and Great Hall for dining crowned
by domes that framed the vista of Inigo Jones's
Queen's House. The design of the Great Hall
was begun in 1698 and by 1704 building work
was completed though it was not until 1726 that
Sir James Thornhill finished the painting of the
interior that was to make the Hall the most
splendid of its kind in England. The dome, over
the vestibule to the Great Hall was built to the
design shown here save that a few details, such as
the roof of the lantern, differ. The upper of the
two tiers of the drum is shown on the elevation,
the clustered columns of the lower stage are
shown on the plan. Wren was a master of skyline
architecture as is proven by the spires to his City
churches. But domes are arguably the most
difficult of all architectural elements to design
and to the purist, Wren's Greenwich domes
considered by themselves, are not completely
satisfactory. As part of a huge formal
composition seen from the River Thames, they
are, however, magnificent.

Lit: J. Summerson, *Architecture in Britain, 1530 to
1830*, Harmondsworth, 1963, pp. 143-4, 173

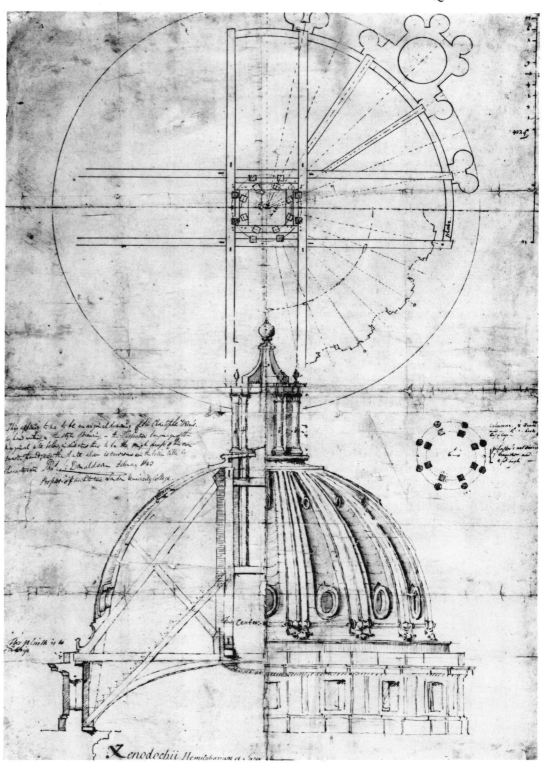

13 Sir Christopher Wren (1632-1723)
Design for the church of St Stephen Walbrook,
City of London, *c.* 1671
Half-sections looking east, to a scale of
approximately 1 1/16 inches to 1
foot
Pen (14½ × 20⅛) (370 × 510)
Provenance: Christopher, son of Sir Christopher
Wren (1675-1747); 1749, 3rd Duke of Argyll;
1761, 3rd Earl of Bute; sold by 3rd Marquess of
Bute, Sotheby's lot 13/44, 23 May 1951

Built on the west side of Walbrook Street in the
City of London, 1672-9, St Stephen's is the most
majestic of the parish churches, about forty five
in all, built by Wren after the Great Fire of
London of 1666.

The cross-sections were taken at two points
looking east: through the crossing (left hand side)
and through the nave (right hand side). They
reveal Wren's draughtsmanship at its most
economic, for this austerely drawn preliminary
design is the solution to the problem of how to
join an aisled nave to a domed crossing while
supporting the dome on eight arches of equal
span. Within a plan that is a plain parallelogram,
Wren defined aisles and transepts by sixteen
subtly spaced Corinthian columns of equal
height, eight of which support the dome. The
solution here can be seen as a trial run for the
vaster and more complex similar problem that
faced Wren in the design of St Paul's cathedral.

St Stephen's Walbrook was damaged by
bombing in 1941 and restored ten years later.

Lit: J. Summerson, *Architecture in Britain, 1530 to
1830*, Harmondsworth, 1963, pp. 125-6; K.
Downes, *Sir Christopher Wren*, catalogue of an
exhibition, London 1982, p. 65

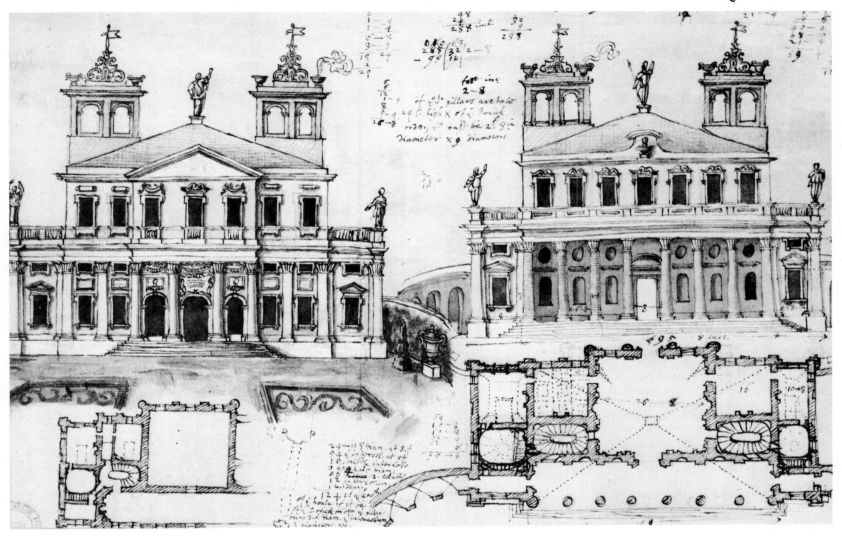

14 John Talman (1677-1726)
Design for a villa near Hampton Court Palace,
London, c. 1699
Sketch plans & elevations
Pen & coloured washes (18¾ × 13½) (220 × 340)
Provenance: Probably part of an album of J. and
W. Talman drawings presented to the RIBA in
1835 by J. W. Hiort and subsequently
dismounted. Other of the drawings from the
album have the border of double red lines that
indicates that they were once in the collection of
Lord Burlington (see no. 11 for Burlington-
Devonshire provenance)

John Talman, son of William Talman (1650-
1719), Comptroller of the Royal Works, was best
known as a collector of 'all that can be called

curious' rather than as a practising architect. As
far as is known none of his designs were ever
built. One of his unrealised schemes was for a
'Trianon' or villa on the south bank of the River
Thames opposite the royal palace of Hampton
Court. Probably intended as a quiet refuge for
William III from the formalities of court life it
was one of several designs for the same site
proposed by both John and William Talman.
The King's death in March 1702 put an end to
such projects.
   The use of an Italian Baroque style by John
Talman for his design is explained by the many
years that he spent in Italy. Many of his designs
have a bizarre quality about them and features
such as chimneys disguised as urns, a multitude
of sculpted figures in heroic poses and the

general air of being well garnished with
architectural bric-a-brac characterise some,
though not all, of his designs for architecture.
Talman's use of colour washes on architectural
drawings was, in England, novel and must have
come from his observations abroad.

see Plate II

Lit: H. Colvin, *Royal Buildings*, London, 1968,
pp.27-29

15 Sir James Thornhill (1675-1734)
Design for the mural decoration of a staircase for
Thomas Highmore
Sketch elevation
Sepia pen (17 × 12¼) (430 × 310)
Provenance: ?; presented to the RIBA by
T.L. Donaldson, in 1876

As a boy of fourteen, Thornhill was apprenticed
to Thomas Highmore, the King's Sergeant
Painter and worked for him until 1703. When his
master died (in 1720) Thornhill succeeded to his
post and was in that same year knighted – the
first British artist to be thus honoured.

A prolific draughtsman with a fund of ideas
and a wide knowledge of mythology and
allegory, Thornhill's sketch for the mural
decoration of a staircase is typical of the kind of
preparatory drawing he made for his decorative
schemes. Based on Homer, it shows (on the right
hand wall) the poet dictating the Odyssey to
Calliope, the muse of epic poetry, while on the
ceiling Pallas Athene reasons with Zeus in favour
of Odysseus. On the drawing Thornhill notes
alternative iconographical programmes based
on the classics and it is interesting to observe
both the way he planned his schemes and his
characteristic use of a theatrical Baroque style
that was rare among English painters. His most
important decorative work was the Great (or
Painted) Hall at Greenwich Hospital (1701-27).
Its complex allegory was sufficiently baffling to
the spectator for Thornhill to publish, in 1730,
An Explanation...

From 1715, Thornhill practised also as an
architect and his best known building is Moor
Park in Hertfordshire (1720-8), built in an
English Baroque style. Others of his architectural
works, including his own house in Dorset, were
tempered by the Neo-Palladianism that was
superseding Baroque.

Lit: E. de N. Mayhew, *Sketches by Thornhill in the
Victoria and Albert Musuem*, London 1967, *passim*.;
E. Croft – Murray, *Decorative Painting in England,
1537 – 1837*, I, London, 1962, pp. 69-78, 271

16 *Attributed to* Antonio Galli Bibiena (1697-1774)
Design for a stage set depicting royal apartments,
c. 1728
Perspective
Sepia & wash (15 × 16¾) (380 × 425)
Provenance: ?: bequeathed to the RIBA with
many other stage designs by Sir John
Drummond Stewart in 1838

Antonio was a member of the Galli Bibiena
family that dominated the field of stage and
theatre design on the continent of Europe from
the 1680s to the 1780s. Ferdinando (father of
Antonio) introduced the *modo di vedere le cose per
angolo* in which the perspective, instead of being
designed along a central axis, was constructed on
one or more diagonals. The *scena per angolo* seen
here has low vanishing points, left and right off-
stage, producing an arrangment more flexible
and more complex that the static and
symmetrical compositions of earlier designers.
Antonio's design for apartments for a royal
personage (the drawing is inscribed, by another
hand, *apartamenti Reali*) fully expresses the
extravagant and exuberantly theatrical nature of
Baroque.

Lit: W. Jeudwine, *Stage Designs*, London, 1968,
p. 22 *et passim*.

Elevation of Chiswick House, London drawn by Henry Flitcroft to
Lord Burlington's design, *c.* 1726.

Neo-Palladianism

Inigo Jones (1576-1652) and John Webb (1611-1672) introduced the Palladian style into England; Colen Campbell and Richard Boyle, 3rd Earl of Burlington, were Neo-Palladians who after an interval of fifty years revived that style. The beginnings of the revival are marked by the publication by Campbell, in 1715, of the first volume of *Vitruvius Britannicus* in which a hundred plates with text advocated the superiority of Palladio and Inigo Jones over the 'affected and licentious' forms of the Baroque. As a propagandist exercise *Vitruvius Britannicus* (followed by further volumes in 1717 and 1725) was extraordinarily successful and was too, an effective advertisement for Campbell who, naturally enough, included some of his own designs. Also published in 1715 was the first instalment of Giacomo Leoni's translations of Palladio's *Quattro Libri dell'Architettura*, one of the textbooks of the Palladian revival. With *Vitruvius Britannicus*, it aroused the attention of the young Lord Burlington to a cause of which he was to become the leading protagonist. His visit to Italy in 1719 especially to study Palladio's works led to his discovery, in the stables of the Villa Maser, of Palladio's drawings of the Roman Baths. These he purchased and on his return to England, bought from John Talman a large collection of drawings by Inigo Jones and John Webb together with the drawings by Palladio that Jones had acquired in Italy in 1614. These drawings became Burlington's chief source for a Neo-Palladian architecture that was sometimes more 'correct' than the originals.

Chiswick Villa (*c.* 1723-9), designed for himself, is Burlington's masterpiece. 'An architectural laboratory, a collection of expositions and experiments' it combined elements from Palladio, Scamozzi, Jones and Webb. The York Assembly Rooms of 1731 was the culmination for Burlington of a decade of architectural activity and, the character of English Neo-Palladianism established, the impetus now passed to Burlington's disciple, William Kent. The best known of Kent's works including Holkham Hall, Norfolk, 1734-65 and Horse Guards, Whitehall, London, built 1750-9, were Neo-Palladian. But, less constrained than his master, Kent ventured into an unantiquarian Gothic (a gatehouse at Hampton Court Palace, 1732, was his first essay) that established him as the inventor of English Rococo Gothick. By about 1755, Vardy in his alternative designs for Milton Abbey could without embarassment offer Neo-Palladian or Gothic. The Neo-Palladian hegemony was over.

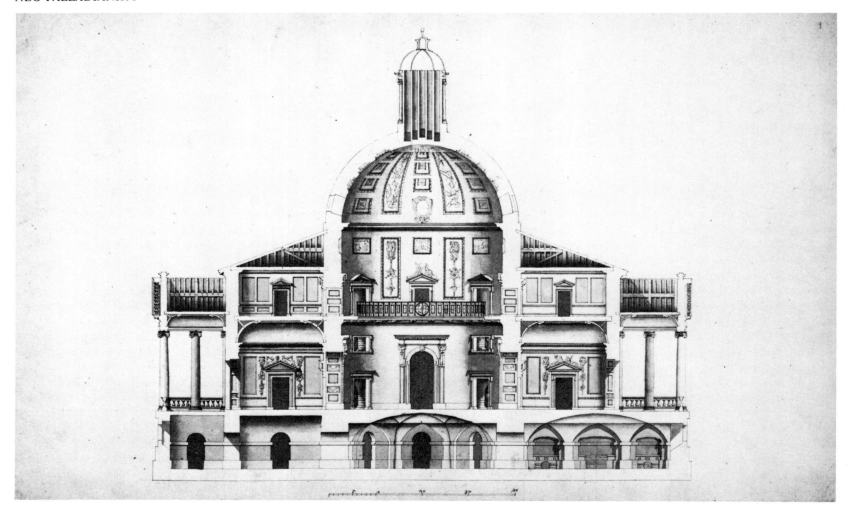

17 Colen Campbell (1676-1729)
Design for Mereworth Castle, Kent for the Hon.
John Fane, *c.* 1720
Section, to a scale of 1/10 inch to 1 foot
Pen & wash (12¾ × 18½) (325 × 470)
Provenance: in 1966 a large collection of Colen
Campbell's drawings was found in two Yorkshire
country houses, Newby Hall and Studley Royal,
and since both houses had belonged to the
amateur architect Sir Thomas Robinson
(1738-1786) it seems that he must have bought
them after Campbell's death. These drawings
were purchased for the RIBA by the Wates
Foundation in 1966

Campbell, a Scottish laird, and a lawyer before
he turned to architecture, based his designs for
Mereworth Castle on Palladio's Villa Almerico
('la Rotonda') at Vicenza. He may have known

that famous villa from his travels in Italy and he
would certainly have owned a copy of Palladio's
Quattro Libri dell' Architecttura in which the design
for la Rotonda was published. There are, though,
some significant differences: Campbell's steeper,
ribbed dome is more Baroque than Palladio's,
and, for the English climate, Campbell raised the
lantern, making it blind so as to conceal the very
necessary chimney flues carried up between the
inner and outer skins of the dome. There are
dimensional differences too: the 80 × 80 feet of
Palladio's villa becomes 90 × 90 feet at
Mereworth. And by having stairways to the north
and south porticos only, Campell broke with the
bi-axial symmetry of Palladio's entrances on four
fronts. This resulted in differences in the plan of
the interior. Moreover, Campbell set Mereworth
in a moat bridged from the two entrance porticos.

By 1723, the shell was complete and

Campbell's Mereworth Castle was thus the first
fully Neo-Palladian building in England. The
decoration of the inside, already elaborately
planned, grew more sumptuous still after Fane's
marriage in 1732 to Lady Mary Cavendish. The
section shown here was one of at least three
variants that Campbell drew up before he
produced the design, published in his *Vitruvius
Britannicus*, volume III, 1725.

Mereworth Castle, its moat filled in at some
time during the 19th century, exists still and is
lived in privately.

Lit: J. Harris, *Colen Campbell, Catalogue of the
Drawings Collection of the Royal Institute of British
Architects*, Farnborough, 1973, pp. 7-9, 14; J.
Harris, *The Palladians*, London, 1981, pp. 66-7

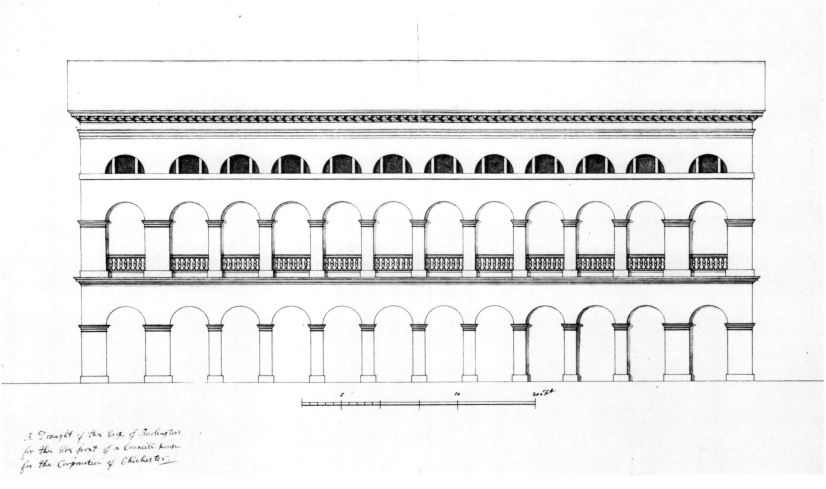

A Draught of the Earl of Burlingtons for the side front of a Councill house for the Corporation of Chichester

18 Richard Boyle, 3rd Earl of Burlington and 4th
Earl of Cork (1694-1753)
Design for the Council House, Chichester,
Sussex, 1730
Elevation of the side, drawn by Henry Flitcroft
(1697-1769), to a scale of 5/32 inch to 1 foot
Pen & wash (12 × 17¾) (305 × 450)
Provenance: not known

Lord Burlington succeeded to his titles and
estates at the age of ten and as a young man
briefly ventured into politics before finding his
true vocation as the leading protagonist of Neo-
Palladianism, a cause to which this foremost of
Britain's 'amateur' architects devoted much of
his wealth and influence.

By 1730, Burlington was accepted as *the*
authority on architectural matters and in that
year the 2nd Duke of Richmond consulted him

over the design of a meeting hall at Chichester, a
project of which His Grace was the principal
benefactor. Two schemes at least were drawn up
under Lord Burlington's direction (the second
and closest to the built scheme is preserved at
Chatsworth House, Derbyshire). However, the
architect who carried out the work was Roger
Morris (1695-1749) and what was built was 'the
perfect example of Palladian ideas applied by a
man who did not know what on earth to do with
them. The building is jolly and friendly but
could have been done as well by the local
bricklayer' (I. Nairn and N. Pevsner, *Sussex*,
Harmondsworth, 1965, p. 172). Burlington's
design shown here is far from jolly and friendly,
it does, though, show his devotion to Palladio.
The austerely organised twelve-bay elevation
uses a number of Palladian motifs, like, for
instance, the semicircular window divided into

three lights that Palladio derived from his study
of the antique Baths of Diocletian in Rome. The
closely-set arched openings of the lower storeys,
Burlington may have adapted from Palladio's
project for the reconstruction of the Ducal Palace
in Venice, *c.* 1578, the design for which Lord
Burlington owned together with other Palladio
drawings.

Lit: H. Burns, L. Fairbairn and B. Boucher,
*Andrea Palladio 1508-1589, the Portico and the
Farmyard*, catalogue of an exhibition, London,
1975, fig. 279 reproduces the proposed design
for the Ducal Palace, Venice; J. Harris, *The
Palladians*, London 1981, fig. 62 reproduces
Burlington's reduced design for the Chichester
Council House (Chatsworth B.16)

19 William Kent (*c.* 1685-1748)
Design for a new House of Lords, Westminster,
London 1735
Plan with laid-out wall elevations of the interior,
to a scale of ⅞ inch to 10 foot
Pen & sepia wash (19 × 14⅛) (480 × 360)
Provenance: ? ; presented by J. D. Crace 1931

Said to have begun his career as a coach painter,
Kent went on to become a history painter and
designer of furniture and interiors before turning
to architecture and landscape gardening. His
amiability, talent and hard work secured him
high patronage and in particular that of Lord
Burlington. It was through Burlington that Kent
received an appointment in the Office of Works,
becoming Master Mason and Deputy Surveyor in
1735. In that year Kent prepared this design, one
of several unexecuted schemes for new
Parliamentary buildings.

Here, Kent proposes a top-lit rectangular
chamber with a throne alcove at the south end
and galleries on four sides. As Burlington's
protegé, Kent was strongly influenced by his
patron's Palladian ideals. It is interesting to
speculate as to which of Palladio's buildings Kent
turned to for inspiration. Howard Colvin has
suggested the basilica (Palazzo dell Ragione) at
Vicenza as a source for some of the features. On
the blank spaces of the sheet are Kent's
characteristic doodles. As well as designs for
ornamental vases and a lion and unicorn device,
there is a sketch of the ceremony of presenting
the Speaker of the Commons to King George II.
Kent notes: *January ye 23 1735, the King came to ye*
house of Lords /[with] *10 other*[s] [to meet] *a speaker*
for ye house/of Commons Mr Onslow was/at ye Barr &
ye black rod [chief Gentleman Usher] *stood by*
him/Duke of Bolton held ye cap of mentenance/Lord
Ownsly ye Sword of State/Duke of Montague & Duke of
Richmond/Duke of Ancaster Lord great Chamberlain
with his rod.

Lit: H. Colvin, *Royal Buildings*, London, 1968, p.35

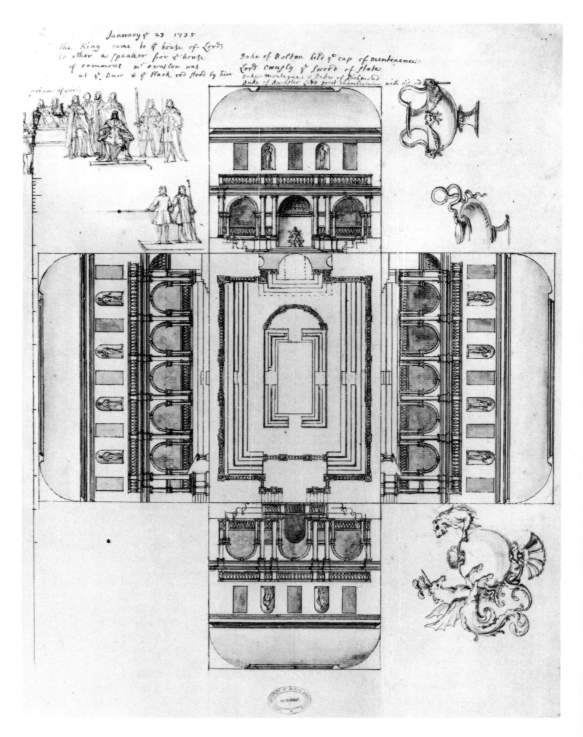

20 John Vardy (died 1765)
Alternative designs for the rebuilding of Milton
Abbey, Dorset for the 1st Lord Milton, *c.* 1755
Elevations, drawn to a scale of 13/16 inch to 10 feet
Pen & sepia wash within a single-ruled border
(11⅛ × 12⅜) (335 × 365)
Provenance: Milton Abbey Collection, purchased
in Dublin, 1931

One of William Kent's most faithful disciples and
a colleague in the Office of Works, Vardy's best
known work as a private architect is Spencer
House, Green Park, London (1756-65).

An earlier commission was for a new house at
Milton Abbey that, once a monastery, had been
since the Dissolution in private hands. Joseph
Damers, a local man, bought the estate in 1752,
acquired an Irish peerage the next year, then
married a daughter of the Duke of Dorset and
later became Earl of Dorchester.

Vardy's alternative designs were both for a
seven-bay, two-storey building with single-bay
wings. The Palladian design is entirely
symmetrical and has pavilion wings while the
Rococo-Gothic design has assymetrical wings of
which the single-storey gabled one is in a style
'earlier' than the rest which is mainly Gothic
Tudor. As it turned out neither of Vardy's
designs was built but in 1769 (four years after
Vardy had died) William Chambers was asked to
revise and build the Gothic design. He did so,
enlarging and regularizing Vardy's design, but it
was not an enjoyable task for neo-Gothic was a
style alien to him: he later wrote with regret of
having built 'a cursed Gothic house for this
unmannerly Imperious Lord who treated me, as
he does everyone, ill'. Nevertheless, Milton
Abbey is one of the finest Georgian Gothic
country houses and exists still (as a boarding
school).

Lit: J. Harris, *Sir William Chambers*, London, 1970,
pp. 58-61

Early Neo-Classicism

Whereas Lord Burlington's classicism took its inspiration from Palladio and other interpreters of antiquity, the Neo-Classicism of the mid-eighteenth century was inspired by the newly discovered and immediate examples of Greek and Roman art and architecture. It was this empirical approach to the monuments themselves that gave Neo-Classicism its strength and style.

The origins of Neo-Classicism are to be found in France and Italy. In Rome Piranesi produced from 1743 his influential sets of etchings which presented archaeological reconstructions of Roman buildings more splendid than the originals had ever been; at the same time he was in contact with the French Academy in Rome which was in the 1740s and '50s a training ground for the future leaders of French Neo-Classicism. In Paris J.G. Soufflot designed the church of Ste-Geneviève (later to become the Pantheon) where he developed the theme of the Roman bath as a domed cruciform church, creating the great monument of the early phase of the style. In the 1750s English architects became great travellers, visiting the ancient sites of the Mediterranean, and as a result published the series of books that made the English contribution to architectural scholarship of outstanding importance in the second half of the eighteenth century. Robert Wood's *Ruins of Palmyra* was published in 1753; James Stuart and Nicholas Revett visited Greece and Asia Minor from 1751-53, but did not publish the first volume of the *Antiquities of Athens* – which became so influential at the end of the century – until 1762. Robert Adam recorded the remains of Diocletians's Palace at Spalatro in 1757 and published his findings in 1764.

From the 1750s the presence of English architects and artists in Rome became increasingly more common; Adam met C.L. Clérisseau in Paris in 1754 and was in Rome in 1756; William Chambers was in Paris from 1749-50 and spent the following five years in Italy. James Wyatt was in Venice and Rome from 1762-68. In Italy architects came into contact with the latest French and Italian ideas and at the same time copied antiquity at first hand by measuring and drawing the monuments.

In England, Robert Adam and Sir William Chambers dominated the architectural world from about 1760 till about 1790. Chambers's domestic builings are more Palladian in style but his public work, and notably Somerset House in London, 1776-96, is in the pure style of Neo-Classical Paris. Adam's houses – for example Osterley Park, 1763-80, and Syon House, 1762-9, both in Middlesex – are more thoroughly Neo-Classical in planning and effect: his 'Adam Style' aimed at recapturing the Roman style of interior decoration.

Sketch of a moulding and stand by Sir William Chambers, from his Paris Album, 1774

21 Sir William Chambers (1723-1796)
Design for York House, Pall Mall, London, for
the Duke of York, 1759
Section showing proposed interior decoration
Pen & watercolour (18 × 23¾) (460 × 630)
Provenance: Thomas Hardwick; P. C. Hardwick,
by whom it was presented to the RIBA in 1885

Chambers had been a pupil at J. F. Blondel's
École des Arts in Paris from 1749-50, where he
met many young architects such as Peyre and De
Wailly who were to be the leaders of French Neo-
Classicism in the 1760s and 70s. He also became
much influenced by the French designers Le
Geay and Le Lorrain in Rome, where he went in
the autumn of 1750. This Franco-Italian
influence can be clearly seen in this unexecuted
design for the Duke of York, which as John
Harris states, was his 'undoing' as the
conservative Duke preferred 'the orthodoxy of an
uninspired Palladian' – Matthew Brettingham the
Elder. Chambers's facade with an arcade
supporting a giant attached portico would have
seemed very un-English, and his proposed
staircase with its domed colonnade on rusticated
arcades would have been equally startling.
Although much disappointed – for this would
have been his first town house – Chambers went
on to become a distinguished government
architect: he was appointed one of the two joint
Architects of the Office of Works in 1761 and in
1782 the first holder of the new combined office
of Surveyor General and Controller.

   The manner of presentation of the drawing –
showing the section of the new design in ruins as
if it were an existing building – had first been
tried by Chambers in his design for the
Mausoleum of Frederick Prince of Wales, 1751-2
(now in the Victoria and Albert Museum,
London). It is likely that Chambers copied the
idea from Charles L. Clérisseau who often used
this technique. This design is also one of the
earliest English drawings to show a complete
scheme for the interior decoration of a house in
colour – particularly unusual as coloured designs
are a great rarity in England before the 1760s.

Lit: J. Harris, *Sir William Chambers*, London, 1970,
pp.63,225, pl.94; J. Fowler & J. Cornforth,
English Decoration in the 18th Century, London,
1974, p.27, pl.1

see Plate III

22 Sir William Chambers
Design for a nobleman's house, late 1770s
Elevation
Pen & watercolour (24⅜ × 37) (620 × 940)
Provenance: not known

The Parisian Neo-Classical style, so evident in this drawing, dates it to the late 1770s and relates it to the Strand front of Somerset House which Chambers designed in 1776. In 1774, with the prospect of designing Somerset House before him, Chambers went to Paris to 'examine with care and make proper remarks upon' the 'many great things' that had been built there since his last visit in 1754. The results of his 'examination' can be seen in his Paris Album (now in the RIBA Drawings Collection) which contains watercolour drawings of the latest Parisian hôtels and public buildings, which were to have considerable effect upon the work at Somerset House and related projects of this date.

This drawing shows a deliberate change of style away from English Palladianism. There is increased ornamentation in the use of an acanthus frieze, free-standing figures, sculptured pediment and fluted Corinthian pilasters and columns. The facade has also a more three-dimensional movement in the recessed arches and rustication of the ground floor and three-bay centre which projects forward. These are French motifs – as can be seen in Antione's La Monnaie – and French, too, is the manner of drawing. The elevation, which is presented as a cut-out frontal perspective against a cloudy sky, is more deeply modelled with shadows than a comparable English design of this date.

Lit: J. Harris, *Sir William Chambers*, London, 1970, pl. 104

23 James 'Athenian' Stuart (1713-1788)
Topographical drawing of the Erechtheum on
the Acropolis, Athens, Greece, *c.* 1751-53
View from the west showing the Caryatid porch
and the artist sketching
Gouache (10¾ × 15⅛) (265 × 385)
Provenance: Elizabeth Ann Stuart, daughter of
the artist, by whom the 20 views were sold to
Jeremiah Harman, Sale, 12-21 May, 1823. By
1861 they were in the possession of Thomas
Howard of Blackheath, by whose executors they
were presented to the RIBA in 1873

This gouache watercolour of the Erechtheum is
one of twenty similar views of Greek antiquities
by Stuart in the RIBA Drawings Collection. They
were engraved, with measured drawings by
Nicholas Revett, for the *Antiquities of Athens*, which
was the first accurate survey of Greek classical
remains and the principal source book of the
Greek Revival in Britain.

'Athenian' Stuart and Nicholas Revett first
made the proposal to measure and record the
Greek antiquities in 1748. They were supported
by members of the Dilettanti Society in Rome
and money was raised to finance the expedition;
they left Venice together on 19th January 1751
and arrived in Athens on 18th March. They
stayed there, with some intervals, until March
1753, and in spite of an outbreak of plague and
fear of assassination, they measured and drew all
the principal monuments of antiquity. They
returned to England in 1755 to prepare the
drawings for publication, but now their dilatory
methods overcame them. The first volume,
dealing with minor Hellenistic monuments, but
including the influential Tower of the Winds and
the Lysicrates monument, did not appear until
1762, and the second was not actually published
until 1789 – a year after Stuart's death. The
second volume covered the buildings of the
Acropolis and included the engraving made of
this lively view of the Erechtheum: Stuart has
drawn himself sketching in the right-hand
corner. The third volume appeared in 1795 and
the final ones in 1816 and 1830.

Stuart throughout had provided the general
topographical views which were executed in
gouache, a technique he had learnt from Louis
Goupy, the well-known French fan painter, for
whom he had worked as a boy. The gouache
technique, consisting of opaque watercolour
paint mixed with gum and honey, provided
Stuart with a colourful and lively medium whose
effects were close to oil painting.

The publication made both men famous and
leaders of the new 'Greek taste'. Stuart's
indolence, however, and Revett's lack of
ambition prevented them from carrying out a
large volume of work, although Stuart's temples
at Hagley, 1758, and at Shugborough in the
1760s, were the first accurate Greek Revival
buildings in Europe.

Lit: J. Mordaunt Crook, *The Greek Revival*,
London, 1968, pl.5; J. Mordaunt Crook, *The
Greek Revival*, London, 1972; David Watkin
Athenian Stuart, Pioneer of The Greek Revival,
London, 1982.

see Plate IV

24 Robert Adam (1728-1792)
Design for the ceiling for the dining room at
7, Queen Street, Edinburgh, for Lord Chief
Baron Ord, 1770
Plan
Pen & watercolour (18¾ × 24) (475 × 610)
Provenance: purchased in 1960

Robert Adam was the second son of William
Adam and the most distinguished member of
that architectural family. Born and educated in
Scotland he left Edinburgh in 1754 to make the
Grand Tour. In Rome under Clérisseau's
guidance he studied drawing and antiquity and
in 1757 made measured drawings of the Roman
Palace of Diocletian at Split in Dalmatia. In 1758
he set up in practice in London and from about
1760-80 was the most fashionable architect in
England. He created the 'Adam Style' of
decoration, whose motifs were drawn from a
wide range of antique classical and Cinquecento
sources. He is particularly noted for the way in
which he incorporated walls, ceilings,
chimneypieces, carpets and furniture into one
unified decorative scheme.

This ceiling plan is a typical Adam design of
the period just before 1770. Damie Stillman
characterized it as being of the 'central motif'
type; an X-shape emphasizes the centre, with
semi-circular panels at the edges of the square.
The central oval is a painted panel, which played
a large part in every Adam interior, often being
painted by Cipriani, Zucchi or Rebecca. One of
Adam's favourite devices for treating the ceiling
of an apse-ended room was to design an end unit
– semi-circular in shape as in the drawing – in
such a way as to make the central panel a self-
sufficient rectangle. This ceiling is similar in motif
and date to that for the Drawing Room of
Lansdowne House, Berkeley Square, which has
now been re-installed in the Philadelphia
Museum of Art.

Adam designed the Edinburgh house for Lord
Chief Baron Ord, a respectable English judge,
who wrote to Baron Mure of Caldwell in 1770: 'I
am engaged in building a house, which is the
second great operation of human life; for the
taking a wife is the first, which I hope will come
in time; and by being present, I have already
prevented two capital mistakes, which the mason
was falling into; and I shall be apprehensive of
his falling into more, were I to be at a distance.'

The ceiling has, unfortunately, been
replastered, but was executed as the Adamesque
frieze still exists.

Lit: A. T. Bolton, *The Architecture of Robert and
James Adam*, London, 1922, II, pp. 207-212;
D. Stillman, *The Decorative Work of Robert Adam*,
London, 1966, *passim*.

25 George Steuart (*c.* 1730-1806)
Design for Onslow Hall, Shropshire, for Rowland
Wingfield, 1780
Perspective of the house in its park
Watercolour with a grey wash border (15 × 19½)
(415 × 555)
Provenance: ?; purchased in 1954

This unexcuted design for rebuilding Onslow
Hall shows what Howard Colvin calls the
'elegant restraint verging on bleakness' that was
characteristic of Steuart's style. His buildings are
Neo-Classical in taste, usually more severe and
original than this early design.

George Steuart, a Highland Scot from Atholl
in Perthshire, practised as an architect in London
from 1770 but his most important works were in
Shropshire where he had a number of
commissions from the local gentry – notably
Attingham Hall, 1783-85, and the exciting and
original St Chad's Church in Shrewsbury, 1790-2.

Steuart's drawings, with their elegant line and
delicate watercolour washes, are some of the finest
of the 18th century. The RIBA Drawings
Collection possesses two notable sets: for Onslow
Hall and for Stoke Park, Wiltshire. Both were
originally bound in albums as presentation sets for
the client, each sheet elegantly finished with a
ruled wash border. Steuart's design for Onslow
was never executed: it was left to Edward Haycock,
a local architect, to rebuild the house in 1820,
which in turn has been demolished.

Lit: J. Harris, *Georgian Country Houses*, London,
1968, pl.24

see Plate V

25

A classical vignette from George Maddox's sketchbook, *c.* 1819-20

Neo-Classical Fantasies

The Neo-Classical fantasy or capriccio can be defined as an architectural drawing showing some fantastic and unrealisable structure, or antique ornament, often in ruins or over-run by predatory nature. The ideas for these fantasies originated in Italy from two sources – the French Academy in Rome and the overwhelming influence of Giovanni Battista Piranesi (1720-1778). There had been in Rome, from the late seventeenth century, a growing interest in the city's antique past, but this interest was increased in the mid-eighteenth century by the archaeological discoveries at Herculaneum and Pompei. It was Piranesi, however, who coming to Rome in 1740, dramatically heightened this vision of antiquity. In 1743, he published his first set of etchings, *Prima Parte de Architetture e Prospettive*, which depicted fantastic reconstructions of Roman buildings, many of the plates being of 'carceri' (prisons), the subterranean antique fortresses festooned in ropes and chains and cluttered with monstrous tackle. (Piranesi later published a further series of etchings of 'carceri'.) It was this type of etching of the 1740s – or its preparatory drawing – that influenced Challe's capriccio shown in this catalogue. In 1748 came the *Vedute di Roma*, consisting of views of Roman buildings, and in 1756 the *Antichita Romana*. In these works Piranesi, who had been trained as a stage designer, combined two traditions – that of Baroque stage design, as exemplified in Galli Bibiena's work, with that of topographical renderings of architectural landscape.

During the 1740s Piranesi came to be closely associated with the French Academy in Rome and may even have been influenced himself by Jean Laurent Le Geay, who was a student at the school from 1737-42. The students of the school, of whom the most notable were Challe, J.L. Le Lorrain, and E.A. Petitiot, were not only much excited by Piranesi's etchings, but also put their creative energies principally into designing the masquerades for the carnival festivities each year. These masquerades needed elaborate structures and backcloths, the designs for which are shown in surviving etchings and drawings by Lorrain, Challe and Petitot. They are for structures of heroic monumentality, great rotundas, triumphal bridges and Temples des Arts, flanked by obelisks and partly obscured by billowing clouds. These designs were to have considerable effect upon the next generation of French architectural students, Marie-Joseph Peyre, Jean Francois Chalgrin and Jacques Germain Soufflot, who were in Rome in the 1750s and '60s and who became the theoreticians and chief practitioners of French Neo-Classicism. Peyre, who was much influenced by Le Geay's fantasies, produced his influential work *Oeuvres d'Architecture* in 1765. This contained megalomaniac designs for cathedrals, French Academies and other public projects and in turn had a far-reaching influence upon architects of the late eighteenth century and particularly on the work of E.L. Boullée and C.N. Ledoux. Both these architects produced a comparatively small body of built work and are best known for their vast and unrealisable projects: Boullee's set of drawings made in the 1790s to accompany his *Essai sur l'Architecture* and Ledoux's publication of designs for an ideal town in 1806. Their fantasies have lived on to exert a considerable influence in another age, particularly on the designs of English architects of the 1970s.

J. M. Gandy was known as the 'English Piranesi' and his large architectural perspectives are the last examples of the Neo-Classical fantasy genre. They have also, however, much in common with the English Romantic Movement and the epic history paintings of John Martin and J.M.W. Turner.

26 Charles Michel-Ange Challe (1718-1778)
An architectural capriccio of the courtyard of a
castle dominated by two fantastic towers with
gantries
Sepia pen & grey wash over red chalk (11⅜ ×
17⅛) (290 × 435)
Provenance: not known; recorded in the 1855
RIBA catalogue

No other artist copied Piranesi's drawing
technique more closely than Challe and, not
surprisingly, this drawing was formerly attributed
to Piranesi.

Challe was a painter, not an architect, and won
the Grand Prix de Rome in 1741. He studied at
the French Academy in Rome from 1742-49, and
like the other students there at the time became
absorbed in designing sets for festivals and
devising architectural fantasies. There was a close
association between the Academy and Piranesi,
whose new etchings were much admired,
particularly as he designed a fireworks festival for
the Academy in 1746.

In style, subject and technique this fantasy is
very close to Piranesi and must date from
Challe's Roman period. It has the freedom and
dash of his early work and is also similar in style
to another fantasy by him dated 1746 in a private
collection.

On his return to Paris Challe had greater
success with the architectural fantasies he
occasionally exhibited than with his history
paintings, and in 1765 was appointed
'Dessinateur de la Chambre et du Cabinet du
Roi'. This was a post usually given to architects –
its function being to design the various court
festivities, and must have been given to Challe on
the basis of his architectural drawings, which
were quite new to Paris at that time. In 1774 he
designed the funeral of Louis XV, which was
celebrated in Notre Dame – providing not only
the catafalque inside but an elaborate Neo-
Classical screen to cover the whole facade.

Challe never lost his admiration for Piranesi
and completed a translation of Piranesi's work
which was not, however, published. He is noted
for his role in bringing a new genre, the Neo-
Classical architectural fantasy, to Paris and
thereby helping to establish the *style classique*.

Lit: R. P. Wunder, 'Charles Michel-Ange Challe,
a study of his life and work', *Apollo*, LXXXVII,
1968, p.28; W. Jeudwine, *Stage Designs*, London,
1968

27 Etienne-Louis Boullée (1728-1799)
Design for a metropolitan cathedral, 1782
Axial perspective
Signed and dated: *1782 Boullée invenit*
Pen & wash (13 × 24⅞) (330 × 630)
Provenance: Sir John Drummond Stewart, by
whom it was presented to the RIBA in 1838

This perspective is related to Boullée's projects
for a Metropolitan Cathedral, which he intended
to erect on the Mont Valérien near Suresnes, or
on Montmartre, where the Sacré-Coeur was
begun in 1876. It shows a view through the
cathedral, of Greek cross plan and monumentally
classical in style, taken from one of the
symmetrical entrances. The nave and aisles are
barrel-vaulted and coffered and are flanked on
both sides by Corinthian columns.

Boullée turned from designing residences for
an elegant clientele in Paris in 1778, after he had
been involved in legal proceedings, and
concerned himself for the rest of his life with
ideal projects for schemes of public architecture.
He was a reformer interested in the life of the
common people, and in his vast and visionary

schemes rejected the rococo and substituted
instead an ordered immensity as expressed in an
elemental classicism. His numerous designs for
individual buildings were intended to be part of
a comprehensive scheme for an ideal city,
including the city walls and gates, theatres,
libraries, cathedrals, museums and court houses.
Boullée left many drawings for these subjects to
the Bibliothèque Nationale in Paris, together
with his manuscript treatise *Architecture, Essai sur
l'Art*, which they were intended to illustrate.

This drawing is very similar in style to those in
the Bibliothèque Nationale; they are all drawn in
pen with pale and sensitive washes – pink, black
and grey predominating. Although designed in
1782, and differing in detail, it closely relates to
the designs for a Metropolitan Cathedral made
for the *Essai*, which was written during the 1790s.

Since the early 1970s Boullée's vast Neo-
Classical schemes, together with those by his
contemporary Ledoux, have had considerable
influence on the more avante-garde architects
and architectural students in England.

Lit: H. Rosenau, *Boullée's Treatise on Architecture*,
London, 1953, p.15; H. Rosenau, *The Ideal City*,
London, 1974, pp. 93-47; H. Rosenau, *Boullée
and Visionary Architecture*, London, 1976, pp. 14, 37

28 Joseph Michael Gandy (1771-1843)
Design for a new Senate House in St James's
Park, London, 1835
Perspective, with figures lining the carriage-way
leading to the entrance
Watercolour (26½ × 40) (675 × 1015)
Provenance: presented by E. H. Gandy and Mrs
C. Rising in 1951

The old Palace of Westminster burned down on
16th October 1834, a spectacular and momentous
sight that inspired Turner's painting of the
subject, now in the Cleveland Museum of Art.
Equally romantic a vision is Gandy's
extraordinary design for a new parliament
building: a monumental Graeco-Roman palace
set against a sky alight with an immense

conflagration. Gandy exhibited this design at the
Royal Academy in 1835 but it is unlikely to have
been one of the serious competition designs for a
new Palace of Westminster, as the terms for the
new building were not announced until June in
that year. There is, however, an element of reality
about the design that distinguishes it from the
other architectural fantasies he exhibited so
regularly at the Royal Academy from 1789 to
1838. The site – St James's Park – is a real one;
the scheme was highly topical. In the top left-
hand corner are Westminster Hall and
Westminster Abbey, outlined against the fire
and, an unusual feature, in the right foreground
is the plan of the building.

Gandy was an architect but never had an
extensive practice. In 1797 he found employment

as a draughtsman in Sir John Soane's office, and
for the rest of his life was indebted to him for
financial assistance and often made elaborate
perspectives of his designs. He seems to have
been of 'too odd and impracticable a nature to
insure prosperity, and it is said that his life was
one of poverty and disappointment.' Most of his
energies went into painting these large
architectural fantasies which have earned him the
title of 'the English Piranesi'.

Lit: *Dictionary of National Biography*; J. Summerson,
'The Vision of J. M. Gandy' in *Heavenly Mansions*,
London, 1949; G. Stamp, *The Great Perspectivists*,
London, 1982, pl. 32

Late Neo-Classicism

The later phase of Neo-Classicism is characterised by the appearance of many different styles. The architect who epitomises the eclecticism of the period is James Wyatt, called by John Summerson a 'stylistic weathercock who turned with the breeze of fashion'. His designs for Downing College and Ashridge show the variety of his work and two of the important themes of late Neo-Classicism: Roman severity and a rationalised Gothic. Soane was an individualist who was influenced by Laugier, Piranesi and George Dance; Bonomi came from Rome with a smart Continental Neo-Classicism and was much taken up as a fashionable designer of country houses.

In the early 1800s, however, there came another important revival which was an essentially English manifestation of Neo-Classicism. This was the style which has come to be known as the Greek Revival, which had its beginnings in the 'Greek taste' of Stuart and Revett's *Antiquities of Athens* and was slow to establish itself in England for a number of reasons. First there was Revett's lack of ambition and Stuart's unbusiness-like manner; secondly Thomas Harrison's early Greek buildings in Chester had little influence in London, and finally there was the opposition of the 'anti-Greeks': Chambers, James Paine and Robert Adam.

In 1804, however, Thomas Hope became an influential protagonist for the new style, and succeeded in his plea for a pure Greek style for Downing College, Cambridge, as opposed to Wyatt's Roman. This established William Wilkins and the Greek Revival in England, which spread rapidly after 1815 as the acceptable style for all public buildings, although the dogmatically Greek element was replaced by a more decorative Greco-Roman in Decimus Burton's Hyde Park Arch of 1827. This in turn led to such monumentally classical schemes as C.R. Cockerell's Royal Exchange design of 1839, which once more looked to current French practice and marks the end of the Neo-Classical phase.

Sketch of a Greek vase in the house of Don Gaetano M. Sterlini, the English Consul at Agrigento, Sicily, by Sir Robert Smirke, *c.* 1801

29 Sir John Soane (1753-1837)
Design for the 3% Consols Office, Bank of
England, London, 1799
Interior perspective
Watercolour (18 × 23¾) (455 × 605)
Provenance: purchased in 1946

A large collection of Soane's architectural
drawings and all his private and professional
papers are in the Sir John Soane Museum at
12 Lincoln's Inn Fields, the house he designed
for himself in 1792 and which he left to the
nation when he died.

The RIBA Drawings Collection has,
consequently, very few Soane drawings, but is
particularly fortunate to have his work
represented by this interior perspective – not
only because the Bank of England was Soane's
most important work but also because, as John
Summerson says 'while one always think of Nash
in terms of exteriors, one thinks of Soane in
terms of interiors.'

Soane succeeded Sir Robert Taylor as architect
and surveyor to the Bank of England in 1788; his
first interior was the Bank Stock Office of 1792,
his second the Consols Office, which was
designed in 1797 and built from 1798-99. This
perspective was probably made after the
completion of the design in 1799 especially for
exhibition at the Royal Academy in 1800, as it is
signed by Soane: *John Soane Architect 1799* and
dated *September 2nd 1800*. It shows well Soane's
highly individual Neo-Classical style. Soane, like
any English architect at this period, had been in
Rome – in 1778 – and his architecture shows the
Franco-Italian influences of that visit. Piranesi's
views of antique domed interiors, lit by
mysterious rays of light, were caught by Soane in
this design, which also shows his more personal
characteristics: a liking for shallow domes,
clerestory windows, segmental arches and astylar
architecture.
In this interior the conventional forms of the
classical orders have been replaced by incised
lines and mouldings, walls flow smoothly into
vaults, and the cast-iron framework of the glazed
lantern is frankly revealed. These abstract and
forward-looking qualities were not as admired in
his own day as they have been in the 20th
century. Soane had no imitators and his share of
criticism. Unfortunately his superb sequence of
banking halls was destroyed during the
rebuilding of the Bank by Sir Herbert Baker
between 1924 and 1939.

Lit: J. Summerson, *Architecture in Britain 1530-
1830*, London, 1953, *passim*; D. Stroud, *The
Architecture of Sir John Soane*, London, 1961, p.66;
N. Taylor, *Monuments of Commerce*, London, 1968,
pl.2

See front cover

30 Joseph Bonomi (1739-1808)
Design for the decoration of the ballroom at
Montagu House, 22 Portman Square, London,
for Mrs Elizabeth Montagu, 1790
Interior perspective
Watercolour within a ruled & wash border
(29¾ × 37½) (755 × 955)
Provenance: presented on indefinite loan by
Anthony de Cosson Rathbone in 1972

Montagu House was designed by James Stuart
from 1775-1782, but from the late 1770s he
seems to have been an impossible person to do
business with. Mrs Montagu wrote to her agent
in April 1780: 'I speak if not on suspicion but
certain information that since he began my
House he has been for a fortnight together in
the most drunken condition with these fellows'
(the workmen). So, not surprisingly, the
decoration of the great ballroom was not carried
out until after Stuart's death, by Bonomi, on the
basis of this design which he exhibited at the
Royal Academy in 1790.

The room was one of the most outstanding
examples of 18th century English Neo-Classicism.
It ran from the front to the back of the house at
the north-east end of the first floor. The
elliptically vaulted ceiling was decorated with
paintings of Olympus, friezes in imitation of
antique bas-reliefs and bands of intertwining
laurel leaves. The door and window surrounds
were of white marble, while the Roman columns
and piers were of green scagliola with gilded
Corinthian capitals. Scagliola was very much a
Neo-Classical fashion, not used until the late
18th century. It consisted of plaster of Paris
coloured and mixed with pieces of marble and
flint to simulate various marbles. David Watkin
has pointed out that the room must have been
based on Stuart's original decorative intentions
as its decoration does not resemble any of
Bonomi's surviving interiors. Sadly, the house
was burnt out by an incendiary bomb in 1941,
and was not rebuilt after the war.

The drawing has a special importance for the
RIBA Drawings Collection as it shows a view of
No 21 Portman Square, the present home of the
collection and Heinz Gallery, as it was in 1790,
through the window at the far end of the
ballroom.

Lit: J. Fowler and J. Cornforth, *English Decoration
in the 18th Century*, London, 1974, pp. 32, 188,
196, pl. XXXlX; D. Watkin, *Athenian Stuart, Pioneer
of the Greek Revival*, London, 1982, p.49, pl.63

see Plate VI

31 Joseph Bonomi (1739-1808)
Design for Rosneath, Dunbartonshire, Scotland,
for the 5th Duke of Argyll, 1803-1806
Perspective of the garden front
Watercolour (24¾ × 38½) (630 × 980)
Provenance: presented on indefinite loan by
Anthony de Cosson Rathbone in 1972

Joseph Bonomi had been born and trained in
Rome but came to England in 1767 to work for
the Adam brothers for several years. In 1784 he
set up in practice on his own, and is best known
for his radical and original Neo-Classical Church
of St James at Great Packington in Warwickshire.
He did, however, achieve a considerable
reputation as a designer of fashionable country
houses and has the distinction of being
mentioned by Jane Austen in *Sense and Sensibility*:
Lord Courtland wanted to build a mansion and

had three different plans by Bonomi; he was
advised by Robert Ferrars to throw them all into
the fire and to build a cottage instead.

Rosneath is a good example of his somewhat
chaste and severe design; the circular belvedere
on the roof shows the influence of the French
Neo-Classicist, C. N. Ledoux. Note also the
hidden kitchen entrance on the right of the
perspective. It was placed underground so as not
to disturb the classical monumentality of the
main house.

Rosneath was gutted by fire in 1947 and
demolished in 1961.

Lit: Wyatt Papworth in *RIBA Transactions*, 1868-9,
pp. 129-33

32 James Wyatt (1746-1813)
Design for Downing College, Cambridge, *c.* 1800
Perspective of the interior of the proposed
quadrangle looking towards the Chapel
Pen & watercolour within black ruled border
(12½ × 31) (320 × 775)
Provenance: purchased in 1966

James Wyatt was without rival as the most
fashionable architect during the late 18th and
first decade of the 19th century, in spite of, in
John Summerson's words, 'an impudent
contempt for the elementary obligations of a
professional man'. When Chambers died in 1796
Wyatt took over as Surveyor General of the
King's Works, and his reputation as a Neo-
Classicist was established with the Pantheon in
Oxford Street, 1770, Heaton House, Lancashire,
1772, and mausolea at Cobham and Brocklesby.
So it was not surprising that he was consulted as
early as 1784 about the design for a new college
at Cambridge – Downing College. He
recommended at the time that it be a building of
'four fine facades', quadrangular in plan and 250
feet square. The site was finally determined in
1800 and Wyatt officially appointed architect.

The view shown in this beautifully lit
perspective is of the internal quadrangle
surrounded by a Roman colonnade looking
towards the Chapel with its portico, square tower
and shallow domed octagonal cupola. Then, in
1804, the Master of Downing, Francis Annesley,
sent Wyatt's design to his friend and arbiter of
taste, Thomas Hope. Hope produced a
pamphlet criticizing Wyatt's Roman design as
'trite, commonplace, nay even vulgar', called the
tower and cupola 'non-descript', and said 'I
should be grieved, grieved to the heart, to see

such a pile arise.' He felt that Greek Doric, then
rather controversial, was the only style worthy of
serious imitation and hinted that William
Wilkins, who had lately returned from Greece
with drawings of Greek temples, was really the
man for the job. Wilkins's design, Greek Ionic
with a Doric Propylaea, was accepted by the
college in 1806 and is also in the RIBA Drawings
Collection.

Wyatt's design has often been dismissed by
historians as inadequate to the occasion. This
perspective, however, shows his great ability to
compose boldly in simplified masses, a very
architectural skill not always evident in Wilkins's
design. Hope and Annesley were exercising a
literary taste for the latest stylistic revival, and in
so doing failed to see that they already had, in
Wyatt's proposal, one of the most forceful Neo-
Classical designs.

Lit: J. Mordaunt Crook, *The Greek Revival*,
London, 1968, pl.14; D. Watkin, *Thomas Hope and
the Neo-Classical Idea*, London, 1968, pp. 61-64;
D. Linstrum, *The Wyatt Family, Catalogue of the
Drawings Collection of the Royal Institute of British
Architects*, Farnborough, 1974; G. Stamp, *The Great
Perspectivists*, London, 1982, pl.16

see Plate VIII

33 William Wilkins (1778-1839)
Design for a lodge or mausoleum at Stourhead,
Wiltshire, for Sir Richard Colt Hoare, 1815
Perspective showing an obelisk in the background
Pen & watercolour (22½ × 35½) (570 × 900)
Provenance: not known

William Wilkins, a classicist turned archaeologist
and architect, toured Greece, Asia Minor and
Italy between 1801 and 1804 and on his return
soon established himself as a leading protagonist
of the Greek Revival. In 1805 his Grecian design
for Downing College, Cambridge, defeated the
Roman version submitted by James Wyatt, and
not only established the Greek Revival as the
newest architectural fashion but launched
Wilkins on a career which included building the
National Gallery and University College,
London.

This unexecuted design for a lodge or
mausoleum at Stourhead shows Wilkins's
passion for the severe and massive qualities of
5th century Greek architecture as exemplified by
the Theseum and the Doric buildings on the
Acropolis in Athens. Athens had impressed
Wilkins most, as a letter dated April 1803 shows:
'What a spring of joy flooded my deepest
feelings, when it fell to me to see afar the cliff of
Sunium, the relics of the bastions of the Piraeus,
the proud bulk of the Temples, and finally the
very Acropolis itself. With what greedy eyes I
scanned everything.' The drawing also shows
Wilkins's severe draughtsmanship and cool
palette well suited to conveying the Doric style,
and illustrates his ability as a perspectivist –
suggesting the solid geometrical presence of the
lodge, with its Greek cross plan, by the dramatic
shadows cast by the portico and columns.

The main portico, defined by the
superimposed attic storey, has the enlarged
central intercolumniation of the portico of the
Propylaea in Athens, a motif which Wilkins had
used in his design for the Propylaea at Downing
College, and which was not executed there for
lack of funds. The side porticoes were copied
from the cella entrances of Greek temples.

The drawing was exhibited at the Royal
Academy in 1817 (no. 890) as 'Building for the
Park of Sir R. C. Hoare Bart', but was never
executed. There is a letter at Stourhead from
Wilkins dated 1815 claiming payment for
£60.18s for making it.

Lit: J. Mordaunt Crook, *The Greek Revival*,
London, 1968, pl.12; R. W. Liscombe, *William
Wilkins 1778-1839*, Cambridge, 1980, pp.62, 63,
141, 237, 255, pl.30

34 John Buckler (1770-1851)
Topographical drawing of Ashridge,
Hertfordshire, 1822
North-east view of the entrance facade
Watercolour (14 × 19¾) (30 × 500)
Provenance: presented by Basil Ionides in 1938

This view of Ashridge drawn by John Buckler,
the topographical artist, shows the house in 1822
after it had been finished by Jeffry Wyatt. James
Wyatt, Jeffry's uncle, was commissioned by the
Earl of Bridgewater in 1803 and his designs date
from 1807; after James's death in 1813 Jeffry
Wyatt (later Sir Jeffry Wyatville) completed the
job. Ashridge was Wyatt's last great Gothic
house. In his obituary notice the *Gentleman's
Magazine* had claimed Gothic as Wyatt's 'favourite
Order', and with houses such as Fonthill for
William Beckford he had played an important

part in the development of the Gothic Revival in
England. But at Ashridge Wyatt tried to
rationalise Gothic; its symmetrical plan and
repetition of elements made it a building closely
related to the geometrical forms of Neo-
Classicism. Pevsner comments on Ashridge's
spectacular compositon and 'the admirable way
in which Wyatt Jun. has entered into the spirit of
Wyatt Sen'. Wyatt's work of 1807-1813 is seen on
the right of the drawing, with the centrally-placed
chapel in the background. Wyatville added the
entrance porch, tall entrance-hall windows and
square staircase tower behind, as well as the
whole of the east wing on the left.

Wyatt, who often neglected both jobs and
clients, spent weeks in his office at Ashridge.
Jeffry spoke of his stay there: 'While he was
employing himself for so long a time...there were
many other works standing still, which, if he had

divided his time properly, would not have been
the case, but by this management he has always
been in difficulties.'

The RIBA Drawings Collection has 188
drawings by Wyatt and 464 by Wyatville for
Ashridge, making it the earliest fully
documented building in the collection.

Lit: A. Dale, *James Wyatt*, London, 1956, passim;
D. Linstrum, *The Wyatt Family*, *Catalogue of the
Drawings Collection of the Royal Institute of British
Architects*, Farnborough, 1974; J. M. Robinson,
The Wyatts: An Architectural Dynasty, Oxford, 1979

35 Decimus Burton (1800-1881)
Design for the Arch and Screen at Hyde Park
Corner, London, 1827
Perspective
Watercolour (24 × 40½) (610 × 1030)
Provenance: presented by the architect in 1880

The Hyde Park Screen and 'Pimlico' Arch were
originally intended to form a grand exit from the
park towards Buckingham Palace. In this
perspective the Arch stands, as it was built, on
the same axis as the Screen – relating to each
other, the graceful Ionic of the Screen making a
formal preface to the rich Corinthian mass of the
Arch, with its coupled columns and heavy attic.
In 1883 this relationship was destroyed when the
Arch was moved to stand on an axis with
Constitution Hill. Burton had been appointed
architect for the various improvements planned
for Hyde Park in 1825 when he was only twenty-
five. First he designed lodges at Grosvenor Gate,
Stanhope Gate, Cumberland Lodge and Hyde

Park Corner and finally the Screen ('the facade'
as it was called at the time) and the Arch, which
was built in 1828.

It is interesting to note that in the early 19th
century perspectives gradually increased in size –
no doubt to hold their own as exhibitable items
in the Royal Academy Architecture Room. The
magisterial size of Burton's (exhibited there in
1827), and the low viewpoint taken, looking from
Buckingham Palace, help to emphasize the
Roman qualities of the Arch, based as it was on
the Arch of Titus, rather than the more delicate
Grecian screen. The statuary in Burton's design
was not executed. Between 1846 and 1883 the
Arch formed the pedestal for M.C. Wyatt's
colossal statue of Wellington, now at Aldershot.
Adrian Jones's present quadriga, following the
lines of Burton's original proposal in this
drawing, was added in 1912 as a memorial to
Edward VII. On the right of the perspective can
be seen the corner of Apsley House, and through
the screen Westmacott's statue of Achilles.

Lit: J. Summerson, *Georgian London*, London,
1962 ed., pl 34; J. Mordaunt Crook, *The Greek
Revival*, London, 1968, pl. 31; G. Stamp, *The Great
Perspectivists*, 1982, pl. 18

36 Charles Robert Cockerell (1788-1863)
Competition design for the Royal Exchange,
London, 1839
Perspective of the principal facade
Pencil, pen & sepia wash (27 × 50) (685 × 1270)
Provenance: presented by Mrs F. M. Noel,
Cockerell's grand-daughter, in 1930

Cockerell's design for the Royal Exchange
should have been built, and certainly one of the
assessors, Joseph Gwilt, described it as 'a very
extraordinary and fine composition and drawing'.
It was, however, the casualty of one of the most
notoriously mismanaged competitions in
architectural history.

The old Exchange was destroyed by fire in
January 1838. The Trustees announced an open
competition in 1839 for a new building which
should be in the 'Grecian, Roman or Italian
style', with a price limit of £150,000. When the
designs were submitted, the assessors found that
of those capable of being built for that sum,
none were actually practicable, but made a
selection of five as 'works of art' and awarded
premiums to three of them. They then drew up a
list of the three best designs which had exceeded
the price limit; in order of merit, these were by
T. L. Donaldson, H. B. Richardson and David
Mocatta. At this point Cockerell revealed that he
was the prime author of the design entered
under Richardson's name. These three architects
then protested at the committee's decision that
their designs had exceeded the price limit and
were allowed to appoint their own estimating
surveyors. Cockerell made the mistake of seeking
the help of William Tite, an architect and
surveyor who had many connections in the City.
Only Cockerell's design fell within the accepted
price, but the committee prolonged the affair by
inviting Cockerell and Tite to engage in a limited
competition of their own, and eventually voted
in favour of Tite's design by thirteen votes to
seven. It was strongly felt at the time that Tite
had manipulated the result, as he was a friend of
the committee's chairman, and particularly as his
design with its octastyle portico was flat and ·
banal in comparison with Cockerell's.

The unusual feature of Cockerell's design is
the magnificent triumphal arch motif of the main
front. The arch, which is extended to form six
giant Corinthian columns, is both symbolic in its
sculptural presence and functional, as it forms
the entrance to the inner courtyard of the
Exchange. Threading behind the columns is a
frieze which bends inwards through the central
archway to form the Doric colonnade in the
courtyard. To the left in the drawing is Soane's
Bank of England and behind it Wren's church of
St Bartholomew's-by-the-Exchange which
Cockerell himself dismantled in 1841 and rebuilt
in Moor Lane.

C.R. Cockerell considered his Royal
Exchange design to be his best work and hung
this perspective directly above his drawing board
as a permanent office fixture. It inspired his best-
known building, the Ashmolean Museum in
Oxford.

Lit: E. M. Dodd, 'Charles Robert Cockerell',
Victorian Architecture, edited by P. Ferriday,
London, 1963, p.116; D. Watkin, *The Life and
Work of C. R. Cockerell*, London, 1974, *passim*;
G. Stamp, *The Great Perspectivists*, 1982, no. 27

Design for a lodge at Audley End, Essex, from the Thomas Cundy
Record Book, 1816

The Picturesque

The Picturesque Movement was formally begun in 1794 by Richard Payne Knight's *The Landscape, a Didactic Poem* and Uvedale Price's *Essay on the Picturesque*. These were followed in 1795 by Humphry Repton's *Sketches and Hints on Landscape Gardening*. All three books were concerned with a new approach to nature. Knight's was an attack on the Lancelot 'Capability' Brown school of landscaping, with its serpentine lakes and carefully composed clumps of trees. Uvedale Price defined the Picturesque as an aesthetic quality to be distinguished from Edmund Burke's two categories of the 'sublime' and 'beautiful'. Some of these ideas had a direct influence on architecture: Payne Knight had himself built Downton Castle, near Ludlow, in 1774, which was the first irregular castellated building. As applied to architecture the Picturesque does not refer to a particular style of building but to the total effect of the house in its natural lanscape setting, and is characterised by asymmetry and variety.

John Nash was the leading architect of the Picturesque Movement. He was in partnership with Repton from 1795 to 1802, and while Repton 'improved' the estates, Nash made alterations to the houses and designed lodges, cottages and dairies in a Picturesque style. From Payne Knight he derived the idea of an Italian type of house, irregular in plan with a round tower and deep eaves – a style he epitomised in the Villa at Cronkill in Shropshire, 1802.

A series of books on cottages were published during the period 1790-1810. The 'cottage' in its many forms, some thatched, some with porches made of tree trunks, some based on Laugier's Neo-Classical primitive hut, but all varied and irregular, became the architectural set-piece of the Movement.

By 1811 the Picturesque Movement was sufficiently well established to be satirised by Jane Austen in *Sense and Sensibility*: 'I like a fine prospect' said Edward 'but not on picturesque principles. I do not like crooked, twisted, blasted trees. I admire them much more if they are tall, straight and flourishing. I do not like ruined, tattered cottages. I am not fond of nettles, or thistles, or heath blossoms. I have more pleasure in a snug farm-house than a watch tower – and a troop of tidy, happy villagers please me better than the finest banditti in the world.'

The Movement did, however, have far reaching effects upon the architecture of the nineteenth century. For the next hundred years the architect was, in effect, painting a picture as he sketched asymmetrical towers and castle keeps and concocted associational styles. This approach naturally affected architectural perspectives which became larger and more painterly.

37 James Malton (died 1803)
Design for a hunting-lodge in the castle-style,
c. 1802
Frontal perspective
Watercolour (8 × 12½) (200 × 320)
Provenance: purchased in 1957

This appealing design for a hunting-lodge is,
surprisingly, triangular in plan. It was engraved
as plate 14 in Malton's *A Collection of designs for
Rural Retreats as Villas principally in the Gothic and
Castle styles of Architecture*, 1802, a book which
presents most engagingly many of the principal
ideas of the Picturesque Movement. Malton felt
that 'immense piles of regular building' were
'incongruous with the scenery of nature' and
rejected the 'Grecian and Roman mode of
fabrick for more picturesque forms'. He wanted
people to retire to the country to villas (patterns

for which he offered in his book) which should
not be of 'great extent...but capable of
accommodating a few chosen friends with ease
and comfort'.

This particular hunting-lodge, formed on the
'castle construction', accommodates the
reception rooms on the ground floor and is
intended to be built on a 'knoll of ground greatly
declining to the rear furnishing opportunity for a
kitchen and offices in an under story'.

Malton made his living as a painter and
topographical artist. He had been employed as a
draughtsman in James Gandon's office in
Dublin, but never actually practised as an
architect. He did, however, regularly exhibit
architectural designs at the Royal Academy, and
in the preface to *Rural Retreats* offered to furnish
estimates to anyone actually wanting to build any
of the designs in his book – and even

volunteered to carry out the contract. Sadly,
none of these have yet been discovered. He is
best known for his first publication *An Essay on
British Cottage Architecture*, 1798, which established
him as a pioneer of the cottage ornée.

Lit: M. Hardie, *Watercolour Painting in Britain*,
London, 1966, vol. I; J. Harris, *Georgian Country
Houses*, London, 1968, plate 35

38 John Nash (1752-1835)
Design for alteratons to Witley Court,
Worcestershire, for the 3rd Lord Foley, 1805
Perspective of the garden front, drawn by G. S.
Repton
Watercolour (16½ × 28) (420 × 710)
Provenance: purchased in 1960

Thomas, Baron Foley of Kidderminster, was an
industrialist who owed his fortune to the iron-
fields of Shropshire and Staffordshire. He
squandered £40,000 – much of it on Witley
Court, where Nash carried out alterations to an
existing Jacobean house which had been
Palladianised in the early 18th century. He
rebuilt and stuccoed it, added a new wing and
gigantic Ionic porticoes to the back and front.
Here we see the garden front with its
conservatory and huge portico of eight columns,
which Summerson notes is probably the biggest

portico of any country house in Britain. Nash
also redressed the towers with picturesque
Italianate eaves in the manner of his villa at
Cronkill. Witley was again altered by S.W. Dawkes
in 1860 and was gutted by fire in 1937.

This perspective is drawn by George Stanley
Repton (1786-1858), the fourth and youngest son
of Humphry Repton, the landscape architect. He
entered Nash's office when he was 15 and
remained there until about 1820 as Chief
Assistant. He was an excellent draughtsman and
his finely detailed sketchbook in the RIBA
Drawings Collection forms a thorough record of
work undertaken in Nash's office, much of which
has failed to survive.

The Witley perspective shows how close
architectural drawings came at this period to
topographical painting – showing how important
it was to present the total appearance of the
house in its landscape setting.

Lit: C. Hussey in *Country Life*, XCVII, 1945, pp.
1036-9; J. Summerson, *The Life and Work of John
Nash*, London, 1980, pp. 49-50, pl. 19B

79

39 John Nash (1752-1835)
Design for the Double Cottage, Blaise Hamlet, Somerset, for John Scandrett Harford, 1810-11
Perspective, with figures seated under a lean-to, set in a landscape, drawn by G.S. Repton
Pen & wash (10¼ × 14½) (260 × 370)
Provenance: Guy Repton bequest, 1935

The Double Cottage was one of nine picturesque dwellings designed by Nash for Harford, the Quaker banker, at Blaise Hamlet. Nash had already designed an orangery and dairy at Blaise Castle House, and when Harford wanted to build accommodation for pensioners on his estate, it was Nash who suggested to him that a more humane way of providing for old people was to give each his own separate cottage, grouped in a secluded spot around a village green. The result is the finest example of picturesque layout and design in the early 19th century.

Each cottage differs from any other: some roofs are pyramidal and thatched, some gabled, some hipped and gabled in tile, as in this example. They are cottages for country folk and have the ideal, almost fairy-tale characteristics of country life such as pigeon houses and garden seats, as here. But although varied in design, they are unified by being all built of rubble masonry, with canopies of tile or thatch and tall, picturesque brick chimneys.

This perspective, drawn up for presentation by G. S. Repton, shows the architect's view of the Picturesque as opposed to the artist's. In the RIBA Drawings Collection is a lithograph of Blaise Hamlet drawn by the artist Joseph Horner. Horner's sketches, deriving from Gainsborough's tumble-down cottages, are far closer to the rustic spirit of cottage life. Repton's cottage is clean and new, almost geometric in its form, and fails to convey the textures and irregularities of rubble, tile and weatherboarding.

Lit: J. Summerson, *The Life and Work of John Nash*, London, 1980, pp. 54-55

40 *Attributed to* James Gillespie Graham (1776-1855)
Design for a Scottish mansion in the castle style, *c.* 1807
Frontal perspective
Pen & watercolour (13¾ × 22) (355 × 560)
Provenance: purchased in 1958

Gillespie Graham was a Gothic Revival architect who had an extensive practice in Scotland, specialising in Gothic churches and castellated country houses. He was the leading practitioner of the picturesque 'castle style' mansion in the second and third decades of the 19th century – a place he was gradually to lose to William Burn. The picturesque movement was slow to develop in Scotland: there architects built mansions in the castle style but imitated the symmetrical patterns of Roger Morris's Inverary Castle and Robert Adam's Culzean Castle. The first manifestation of *irregular* Gothic was Tullichewan Castle, Loch Lomond, designed by the English architect Robert Lugar in 1808. Gillespie Graham's Culdees Castle, Perthshire, 1810, shows the influence of Lugar, and from this date he produced a series of mansions which, although basically symmetrical in plan, were given a picturesque outline by the addition of a large round tower on one side. This design is one sheet of several orginally bound into a presentation album with the watermark Whatman 1807. Neither the album nor the drawings are signed but have been attributed to Gillespie Graham on stylistic grounds. The design has many of the characteristics of his style: the circular drum tower on one side, with attached towerlet, square hood-mouldings over coupled Gothic windows, and the drop in level on the 'garden' side of the house. The draughtsmanship is naive, although precise in style, and unlike Gillespie Graham's own hand – indicating that the design is more likely to be the work of an assistant. It is not known if it was ever executed.

Lit: J. Macaulay, *The Gothic Revival 1745-1845*, Glasgow & London, 1975, *passim.*

Exotic Sources

By the 1740s one of the by-products of Neo-Classicism was a new interest in exotic styles, together with the Greek and Gothic revivals. In England the fashion for Chinese garden architecture was spreading rapidly and it was at Kew that a firm and objective interest in exoticism was first clearly displayed on a large scale. Sir William Chambers, who created the garden buildings there between 1757 and 1763, had himself visited China as a young man in the 1740s and had, by the end of that decade, acquired a considerable reputation as an amateur sinologist. In 1756 he published *Designs for Chinese Buildings*, which was very influential both in England and on the Continent. In it he calls Chinese buildings 'toys in architecture', meaning small and skillfully produced, explaining that 'as toys are sometimes, on account of their oddity, prettyness or neatness of workmanship, admitted into the cabinets of the curious, so may Chinese buildings be sometimes allowed a place among compositions of a nobler kind'.

Chambers had also included Moorish buildings at Kew, the Alhambra and the Mosque, but it was not until the end of the eighteenth century that there was anything in Britain remotely reflecting the architecture of India: the idea of reproducing Indian styles in England only took shape after the exploration of India by the artist Thomas Daniell, who went there with his nephew William in 1784. Between 1786 and 1793 the Daniells made arduous tours of India and built up a vast stock of drawings of Indian buildings, of which the RIBA possesses a large collection. Back in England they spent thirteen years from 1794 in making 144 aquatints. The finished watercolours and oil paintings, exhibited regularly at the Royal Academy, were all based on their topographical drawings made on the spot, many with the *camera obscura*, and depicted a wide range of Indian buildings, from the Mughal monuments of upper India to the great Hindu temples of the south and the rock-cut temples of western India. These pictures were much collected by people of taste and were used by the architect Samuel Pepys Cockerell when he began to build Sezincote House in 1805. The Indian taste also spread to influence first Repton's and then John Nash's design for the Royal Pavilion at Brighton. It also seems that Frederick Crace who furnished the Pavilion in Chinese taste was interested in Daniells' India, for it was from the firm of Crace and Sons that the RIBA received its collection of Daniell drawings.

A few years later another exotic source developed – drawings by Indian artists made for British residents in India. These were bound into sets and found their way into the libraries of connoisseurs in England, providing a more colourful and detailed record of decoration and ornament for the architect to draw on, should he, as Repton did, need 'new sources of beauty and variety'.

Design for a garden pavilion at Kew Gardens, London. *Attributed to* John Henry Muntz (1727-1798), 1750

41 Sir William Chambers (1723-1796)
Design for the Pagoda, Kew Gardens, London,
1761
Elevation
Pen & watercolour (24 × 17) (610 × 430)
Provenance: 3rd Earl of Bute, sold Sotheby's
May, 1951; purchased by the RIBA in 1966

Between 1757 and 1763 Chambers was
employed by Augusta, the Dowager Princess of
Wales, to lay out the gardens at Kew Palace. Only
five of the twenty-five buildings erected there
survive: the Orangery, the Ruined Arch, the
rebuilt temples to Bellona and Eolus – and the
Pagoda.
   The Pagoda, standing 163 feet high, was the
most ambitious and splendid chinoiserie garden
structure in Europe. Chambers himself says the
design was an imitation of the Chinese Taa
Pagoda engraved in his *Designs for Chinese
Buildings*, 1756, but there is little doubt that it was
chiefly inspired by the so-called Porcelain Tower
of Nanking as engraved in Jan Nieuhof's *An
Embassy from the East India Company of the United
Provinces to the Grand Tartar Cham Emperor of China*,
1669. Like the Nanking pagoda this design is
octagonal with the same ground storey and nine
storeys above, tapering slightly. Chambers notes
that 'all the angles of the roofs are adorned with
large dragons, being eighty in number, covered
with a kind of thin tin glass of various colours,
which produces a most dazzling reflection, and
the whole ornament at the top is double gilt.'
Sadly the Pagoda has now lost its glitter of glazed
tiles and its ever-watchful dragons.
   This elevation is the second or revised design
finalised in 1761, and differs from the engraved
version, the original drawing for which is with
the manuscript of the *Plans, Elevations, Sections and
Perspective Views of the Gardens and Buildings at Kew
in Surrey*, 1763 in the Metropolitan Museum of
Art, New York. It is also likely that the
watercolour has faded: there are traces of scarlet
and gold which no doubt would have originally
been much brighter to convey the 'dazzling
reflections' of Chambers's Eastern sources.

Lit: A. Rowan, *Garden Buildings*, London, 1968,
pl. 24; J. Harris, *Sir William Chambers*, London,
1970; P. Conner, *Oriental Architecture in the West*,
London, 1979

42 Thomas (1749-1840) and William (1769-1837) Daniell
Topographical drawing of the Palace at Rhotas, Bihar, India, made in late January 1790
Watercolour (14 × 23¼) (355 × 590)
Provenance: the Daniells' drawings were acquired by Frederick Crace (1779-1859) when Thomas Daniell's collection was dispersed after his death in 1840; they were presented to the RIBA by John Dibblee Crace in late 1889 or in 1890 with 24 drawings by Indian artists, bound in seven volumes

This drawing is one of the more finished watercolours produced by the Daniells on the first of their two tours of India. Their first journey, lasting from August 1788 to late in 1791, took them to the north of India. They had travelled up the Ganges to Cawnpore by budgerow, or river barge, halting at every picturesque spot with a ruined temple or palace. From Delhi they went northwards to the Himalayas and spent April 1789 drawing the mountain scenery. In October 1789 they began the return journey to Calcutta and in December made a detour to Jawnpur. Leaving the river they spent the cold weather of 1790 wandering through the jungly hills south of the Ganges, sketching the hill-forts and then making their way back to the river through Bihar, where Rhotas is situated.

Throughout the tours the two Daniells worked relentlessly. At each place they studied any building which interested them and produced a vast number of drawings, some outline pencil sketches, others with sepia or blue-grey washes and some full watercolours. Often it was William's job to operate the camera obscura and to put in the simpler washes, while his uncle did the more complicated and delicate work. This particular watercolour was engraved in *Oriental Scenery*, part III, plate 2, 'Ruins in Rotas Gur in Bahar, 1 August, 1801'.

Lit: M. Archer, *Indian Architecture and the British*, London, 1968

43 Unidentified Agra or Delhi artist
Topographical drawing of the Mausoleum of
Itimad-ud-daula, near Agra, Uttar Pradesh,
India, *c.* 1828
Interior view
Pen & watercolour, with applied gold paint
(21⅛ × 29⅝) (535 × 750)
Provenance: purchased in 1947 with 8 other
watercolours by Indian draughtsmen.

The cenotaphs of Itimad-ud-daula and his wife
lie in a chamber richly decorated with *pietra dura*
work. The mausoleum had been built in 1626 by
Nur Jahan, wife of the Emperor Jahangir, for her
father, the Persian Mirza Ghiyas Beg who had
received the title 'Itimad-ud-daula' meaning
'Support of the State'. The drawing, by a native
Delhi or Agra artist, is one of many made at the
beginning of the 19th century to supply a
demand from British officials in India for
artistic records of the highly picturesque ruins of
the Mughal Empire. By about 1806 large
numbers of such drawings had been produced
and were often bound in sets and taken back to
England. It is likely that the artists were shown

examples of European architectural drawings as
models. In this drawing the European
convention of perspective is adopted, as is the
double-ruled border, a common feature of 18th
century Venetian drawings. Here, however, the
Indian love of pattern, colour and detail is
stronger and asserts itself in the meticulous use
of scarlet, blue, green and gold to convey the rare
inlaid stones such as onyx, cornelian, topaz and
jasper, and in the decorative treatment of the
ceiling vaulting, pierced screens and patterned
floor.

Lit: M. Archer, *Indian Architecture and the British*,
London, 1968, pl 31

see Plate VII

The Gothic Revival of the 1830s

The Gothic style really never died. It survived in country backwaters; it was used by architects such as Wren and Hawksmoor when architectural good manners required it; it was transformed into Baroque by Vanbrugh, and William Kent wedded it to Rococo. John Vardy's designs for Milton Abbey, *c.* 1755 show his willingness to use Gothic as an alternative to Palladianism. Antiquarianism, literary tastes, sentiment, Romanticism, the Picturesque Movement and patriotism first sustained and then widened its scope. From the 1790s when James Wyatt designed Fonthill Abbey, Gothic became less and less the very occasional alternative to the prevalent style. In 1835 when the competition for the new Palace of Westminster was announced, 'Gothic or Elizabethan' was stipulated. The successful Charles Barry may well have preferred the Italian style and the organisation of the building with its symmetrical plan is certainly Classical. But the tall towers, assymmetrically placed, give a picturesque outline and the wealth of detail designed by A.W.N. Pugin was entirely Gothic. All the same, the new parliament building belongs to the Picturesque period of the Gothic Revival as does Thomas Rickman's competition design for the Fitzwilliam Musuem, 1834. For though the details are studied, the effect is highly picturesque.

The second phase of the Gothic Revival, what Kenneth Clark has called the 'ethical period' began with Pugin. Though he had collaborated with Barry on the Houses of Parliament, he himself described the building as 'All Grecian, sir; Tudor details on a classic building'. Pugin's designs for Scarisbrick Hall, 1836, belong to the very first years of his independent career when his work was 'original, dramatic, unrestrained' and not yet disciplined by the ideas expressed in his *The True Principles of Pointed or Christian Architecture*. Published in 1841, the book showed Pugin's understanding of the connection between the style, construction and function of Gothic architecture and it marks a new chapter in the history of the Gothic Revival in Britain.

Designs for bosses on the library ceiling of Scarisbrick Hall Lancashire, by A.W.N. Pugin, 1837.

44 Thomas Rickman (1776-1841) and Richard
Charles Hussey (1806-1887)
Competition design in Gothic style for the
Fitzwilliam Museum, Cambridge, 1834
Perspectives of the Grand Staircase and of the
Library.
Watercolour (10⅝ × 6¼) (270 × 160) (11⅜ × 6¼)
(295 × 210)
Provenance: presented by Miss Mary A. Lynam
(T. Rickman's great niece) in 1912

A self-taught architect, Rickman came to the
profession after trying both medicine and
commerce. Though he designed an enormous
number of churches, public buildings and
houses, he is probably best remembered as the
author of *An Attempt to Discriminate the Styles of
English Architecture from the Conquest to the
Reformation*, 1817, the earliest systematic treatise
on English Gothic architecture that proposed for
the first time the terms, still widely used,
'Norman', 'Early English', 'Decorated English'
and 'Perpendicular English' for the different
phases of the style.
   This staircase design is in a Decorated English
Gothic style and reveals Rickman's knowledge of
architectural detail of that period. At the same
time that he and his partner Hussey prepared
their Gothic design they also made designs in the
Roman (Corinthian) classical style and Greek
(Doric) classical style. Despite the boldly
imaginative qualities of all three designs, none of
them were successful. The winning entry in the
open competition for the Fitzwilliam Museum
was an opulently Graeco-Roman design by
George Basevi. The museum, (with some
interesting 20th century additions), exists still.

Lit: D. Watkin, *The Triumph of the Classical:
Cambridge Architecture 1804-1834*, catalogue of an
exhibition, Cambridge, 1977, p.41 *et seq*

NEW · HOVSES · OF · PARLIAMENT ·

SOVTH FRONT

45 Sir Charles Barry (1795-1860)
Revised competition design for the New Houses of Parliament, Westminster, London, *c.* 1836
Elevations of north and south fronts.
Sepia pen, grey pen & wash (each 8½ × 12½)
(215 × 315) (Only one is illustrated)
Provenance: presented by C.A.R. Barry (the architect grandson of Sir Charles Barry), in 1938

After the destruction by fire of the Houses of Parliament on the night of 16th October 1834, it was decided to hold an architectural competition for a new building. Of the ninety-seven designs submitted. Charles Barry's scheme won the first prize. His success lay in a well conceived plan and in the collaboration of A.W.N. Pugin to whom is owed the inventive Gothic detail that is so important a part of the new Palace of Westminster. From February 1836 (when the competition result was announced) continous

modifications to the original design were made to meet changing requirements and the elevations shown here were drawn after the competition and before the finalised design. As built, the north and south fronts are shorter, the keep-like Victoria Tower stops the south-west corner and the Clock Tower, not designed in its final form until the mid-1840s stops the north-west corner.

Lit: P. Stanton, *Pugin*, London, 1971, pp. 20-3 *et passim*; M.H. Port (ed.), *The Houses of Parliament*, New Haven and London, 1976, *passim*.

46 Augustus Welby Northmore Pugin
(1812-1852)
Preliminary design for the Great Hall at
Scarisbrick Hall, Lancashire, for Charles
Scarisbrick, 1836
Interior perspective
Pencil & watercolour (17½ × 13¾ cut to the shape
of the roof) (445 × 350)
Provenance: purchased, with other drawings for
Scarisbrick, from St Katherine's College (until
1963, the owners of Scarisbrick Hall) in 1964

Pugin crammed a great deal into a short life:
architect and designer, architectural theorist and
polemicist, his work, after his conversion to
Roman Catholicism in June 1835, was inspired
by a passion for the architecture of the Catholic,
that is, Gothic, past in England. His first
important commission came from Charles
Scarisbrick, an eccentric and wealthy recusant
Catholic who had inherited Scarisbrick Hall in
1833. His family had lived there from at least the
13th century but the house that Pugin was asked
to re-model seems to have been a half-timbered
house of the 16th century that in 1813-16 had
been encased with stone in a Tudor-ish style by
Thomas Rickman. From 1836 to 1845 Pugin
found plenty to add and to re-do.
   It is not clear, though, how much of this
perspective of the Great Hall shows his work and
how much of it is Rickman's. Certainly the
executed design varies considerably except, that
is, for the chimneypiece with its knights in
armour. There are now, for instance, more
windows and the architecture of the timber roof
is different. It is characteristic of Pugin to have
added a table, dresser and chest – all well
garnished with plate – for he was foremost
among the architect-designers of the 19th
century, who in Britain, dominated the
decorative arts.

Lit: A. Wedgwood, *The Pugin Family, Catalogue of
the Drawings Collection of the Royal Institute of British
Architects*, Farnborough, 1977, pp. 74-5 *et seq.*

Monuments of Commerce 1830s-1860s

The Industrial Revolution created a need for new types of building and that need was met by a new kind of architect – independent, often self-made, determinedly professional and, on occasion, prepared to exploit new materials and technology. The cloth mills of northern England, designed in the 1790s, were the world's first iron-framed, multi-storey buildings. The structural problems of market halls, railway stations and exhibition buildings that spanned large, unencumbered floor areas were solved by a daring use of cast, or wrought iron, laminated wood and glass that culminated in Sir Joseph Paxton's Crystal Palace of 1851.

Charles Fowler was a gifted architect with an engineer's ability to handle structure. Hungerford Market (1831-33), designed in an appropriately simplified Neo-Classical style, was a brave example of structural economy in which cast-iron, brick and a laminated tile roofing system were employed.

Mocatta's designs for the stations on the London to Brighton Railway (1839-46) reveal in the rational, shed-like structure of the platform canopies, the influence of his friend Fowler. Fowler had earlier built the great glazed conservatory at Syon House, Middlesex (1827-30) that, by inspiring the series of glasshouses designed by Paxton, led to the design of the Crystal Palace. Though this was followed by other large structures such as Cuthbert Brodrick's Leeds Corn Exchange (1860) of 190 by 136 feet and crowned by an iron, timber and glass dome, further advances in terms of 'megastructure' had to wait upon the invention of mechanical and electrical services (main drainage, elevators, telephones, air-conditioning and so on) as yet unheard of.

Style had not been Paxton's concern in the design of the Crystal Palace. The direct descendant of train sheds and glasshouses, its form and appearance were determined by function, structure and materials. However, style was a consideration in the design of most commercial buildings. Gothic, associated with churches and conservatism did not find acceptance until the 1860s. Italianate or Franco-Italianate in various manifestations were approved, suggesting, as they might, a degree of sophisticaton, 'modernity' and respectability. For interiors, Louis Quatorze or 'florid Italian', that is, a mixed Franco-Italian Renaissance style that lent itself to an opulent, all-over decoration, became very popular for commercial interiors. First used by Benjamin Wyatt for two London houses (Lancaster House and Apsley House) in the 1820s, P.C. Hardwick used it for the interiors of the Great Western Hotel, London (1852) and R. L. Roumieu, adding a touch of Louis Quinze, for a Bond Street shop (1853).

Perspective of the entrance to 1 and 2 Hammond Court, City of London, by George Aitchison, c. 1853.

47 Charles Fowler (1792-1867)
Design for Hungerford Market, Charing Cross,
London, *c.* 1832
Perspective of the Galleries
Watercolour (21¾ × 16⅞) (550 × 430)
Provenance: presented by the architect in 1835

Hungerford Market, demolished in 1862 and
replaced by Charing Cross railway station, was
Fowler's finest work. Other large, covered
markets designed by him include Covent Garden
Market in London (1826-30) and the Lower
Market, Exeter (1834-7, demolished 1942), and
all reveal Fowler as a pioneer designer of what
was then a new building type. His belief that 'the
proper excellence of architecture is that which
results from its suitableness to the occasion'
places him among the early rationalists and his
structural principle of 'enough for security and
not more than enough', alongside the leading
engineers of the time.

The site of Hungerford Market lay between the
Strand and the River Thames in London and the
market, when built, was over 390 feet long. At
the Strand end were shops and colonnades, in
the centre a large covered market hall and,
towards the river, a wholesale fish market flanked
by two taverns, with a wharf and stairs for
loading and unloading fish. Fowler's perspective
shows the view from the galleries above the fish
market (and a fish porter with his characteristic
hat is among the figures). The simple Tuscan
columns were of granite, the walls were one-and-
a-half bricks thick, the corner pavilions were
strengthened by interior cast iron columns at the
corners and roofed with a laminated tile system.
When a covered roof was needed for the fish
market, Fowler designed a remarkably advanced
free-standing, cast iron structure with a double-
butterfly roof.

Lit: J. Taylor, 'Charles Fowler: master of
markets', *Architectural Review*, CXXXV, 1964, pp.
174-82; J. Taylor, 'Charles Fowler: a centenary
memoir', *Architectural History*, XI, 1968, pp. 57-74.

Galleries, Hungerford Market
Chas. Fowler, architect

48 David Mocatta (1806-1882)
Design for Reigate railway station, Redhill, Surrrey, 1840
Perspective of the platform front
Pen & watercolour within a single-ruled border
(14 × 20⅝) (355 × 525)
Provenance: not known

The Railway Age began in Britain, when the first of thousands of railway stations – the Liverpool & Manchester railway station at Crown Street, Manchester – opened in 1830. A host of railway companies were set up in the following years including the London, Brighton & South Coast Railway Company who employed David Mocatta to design (between 1839 and 1846) a number of stations in Sussex and Surrey, including those at Brighton, Hove, Hassocks, Haywards Heath, Crawley, Horley, Stoat's Nest, Croydon and Reigate, just outside Redhill.

The division between the conventionally designed and constructed booking hall with its ticket office, waiting room, station master's office and so on and the engineering structure of the train shed that spanned line and platform to keep passengers dry, was established from the beginning. In his design for Reigate railway station Mocatta used a free Italianate style with stuccoed brick construction for the booking hall and timber king-post trusses for the shed. For a country station nothing larger or more elaborate was required.

93

49 Philip Charles Hardwick (1822-1892)
Design for the Coffee Room, Great Western
Hotel, Praed Street, Paddington, London,
c. 1852
Interior perspective
Sepia pen & watercolour (18⅛ × 26¾) (460 × 680)
Provenance: presented by Mrs Lyons in 1923

P.C. Hardwick was a fourth-generation architect
who inherited the family practice much of whose
work was for railway companies such as the
London & Birmingham Railway and the Great
Western Railway. It was for the latter that
Hardwick designed the Great Western Hotel, the

second of the big railway hotels to be built in
London. The first were the twin hotels at Euston
Station designed by his father Philip Hardwick,
1836-40.

The Great Western Hotel stands to the south
of Paddington Station (the terminus for the lines
from Wales and the West of England), designed,
in the main, by the engineer Isambard Kingdom
Brunel. When it was built the hotel was the most
sumptuous in the country and one of the earliest
English buildings designed in the mansarded
French Second Empire style. Among the public
rooms was the Coffee Room which was as
imposing as any in a London clubhouse.

The Hotel still stands but alterations made in

about 1933 swept away all of Hardwick's High
Renaissance interior decoration including, sadly,
those of the Coffee Room.

Lit: N. Taylor, *Monuments of Commerce*, London,
1968, pp. 56-7; H. Hobhouse, 'Philip and Philip
Charles Hardwick, an Architectural Dynasty',
Seven Victorian Architects, ed. J. Fawcett, London,
1976, pp. 40-2

50 Robert Lewis Roumieu (1814-1877)
Design for the interior of Mr Breidenbach's
shop, 157 New Bond Street, London, 1853
Interior perspective
Pen & watercolour (20½ × 27) (520 × 685)
Provenance: presented by J. Fox Jones in 1956

Roumieu's architectural practice reflected the
burgeoning world of London and its suburbs
from the 1840s to the 1860s. He laid out housing
estates, designed churches and schools for new
parishes, and was responsible for a number of
warehouses and other commercial premises.
Critical judgements on his work have in the past
been harsh. Henry-Russell Hitchcock described

Roumieu as an architectural criminal whose
'wild fantasies...are hardly worth considering' but
more recent judgements have been kinder and
some of those works that have survived are being
carefully restored.

Roumieu employed a variety of styles ranging
from a 'terrifying Prussian trabeation' to fanciful
mixed Gothic. For a West End shop for Mr
Breidenbach 'perfumer and distiller of eau-de-
cologne to H.M. The Queen' he used Italianate
arches to define a space made apparently larger
by mirrors and culled the decoration from
French Renaissance sources. Carved and
upholstered chairs, a circular settee with flower
stand, elaborately designed light fittings and

carpet all contributed to an atmosphere of
conspicuous expenditure.

Lit: H. – R. Hitchcock, *Early Victorian Architecture*,
New Haven, 1954, pp. 125, 158; N. Taylor:
Monuments of Commerce, London, 1968, p. 36

see Plate IX

51 Sir Joseph Paxton (1801-1865)
Bird's eye view of the Crystal Palace and its
grounds at Sydenham, Kent (now London)
drawn by J. D. Harding (1798-1863), *c.* 1854
Pencil & watercolour heightened with white
(36¼ × 76⅜) (920 × 1940)
Provenance: presented by the Trustees of the
Chatsworth Settlement in 1973

The seventh son of a Bedfordshire farmer,
Paxton's meteoric rise from gardener's boy to
head gardener to land agent to architect and
landscape architect, business man and politician
fully justified the opinion of *The Times*, London,
obituarist that 'he rose from the ranks to be the
greatest gardener of his time, the founder of a
new style of architecture, and a man of genius.'

The building for which Paxton is best known is
that built to house the Great Exhibition of
Industry of All Nations of 1851. At first the
subject of a competition, when the costs and
construction programme of the two commended
designs were deemed unsatisfactory, another
design was prepared by the Exhibition
Committee. When their design proved even
more costly and the execution of it likely to be
more protracted than the competition designs,
Paxton stepped in with a sketch design on a piece
of blotting paper. It was based on the
conservatory, designed to hold the gigantic
Victoria Regia water lily, that was built for the 6th
Duke of Devonshire at Chatsworth (1849-50). By
now time was running very short, it was June
1850 and the Exhibition was due to open in May
1851. Perhaps through desperation, the
committee agreed to Paxton's proposals, changes
were made to the design, for example to
accommodate a group of elm trees on the site at

Hyde Park, and the building was completed on
time. When finished it was 1840 feet long, 408
feet wide, with an extension at one end of 936 by
48 feet and at its highest point it was 198 feet.

Designed so that its parts were factory-made
and assembled on site, this prefabricated
building presented few problems when it was
moved in 1852 to a site at Sydenham, then just
outside London. It was enlarged by 50% to house
collections of manufactures, geological
specimens, plaster casts, statues and historical
courts. Paxton laid out the grounds with terraces,
flower beds, fountains, cascades and two lakes
with islands decorated with reproductions of
prehistoric animals.

The Crystal Palace survived until 30th
November 1936 when fire destroyed it. James
Duffield Harding painted this bird's-eye view
two years before the building was re-opened by
Queen Victoria in June 1856.

Lit: G. F. Chadwick, *The Works of Sir Joseph Paxton,
1803-1865*, London, 1961, pp. 104-159 *et passim*.

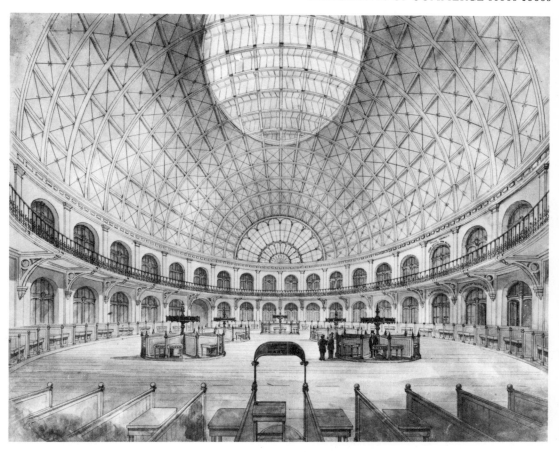

52 Cuthbert Brodrick (1822-1905)
Competition design for the Corn Exchange,
Leeds, Yorkshire, 1860
Interior perpsective
Pen & watercolour (30 × 24¼) (510 × 615)
Provenance: presented by H. Trevor Field in 1940

Cuthbert Brodrick was one of those 19th century
architects who, like, for example, Alfred
Waterhouse and T. E. Collcutt, owed their
success to the architectural competition system.
When Brodrick won the competition for Leeds
Town Hall in 1853 he moved to that city and
went on to design many of its grandest buildings,
three at least of which were won in competitions.

The Corn Exchange in Duncan Street, Leeds,
is considered to be Brodrick's most original
building. Spatially, it is an exercise in curved
geometry: the elliptical plan is crowned by a
partly glazed, elliptical dome, doors and
windows have semi-circular heads and porches
are semicircular in plan. While details such as
roundels continue the curvilinear theme, the

diamond-rusticated masonry of the exterior and
X-bracing to the roof offer a spikey counterpoint.
In execution the interior varied from the
perspective shown here: the pilasters were not
built and deeply moulded architraves were
added to the arched openings. Brodrick's sources
were Franco – Italianate, that is, Italian
Renaissance forms and details re-interpreted by
the French Romantic Classicism of the 19th
century and applied in an independent manner
to a functional building.

Lit: D. Linstrum, 'Cuthbert Brodrick: an
Interpretation of a Victorian Architect', *Journal of
the Royal Society of Arts*, CXIX, 1971, pp. 80-1

The Later Gothic Revival

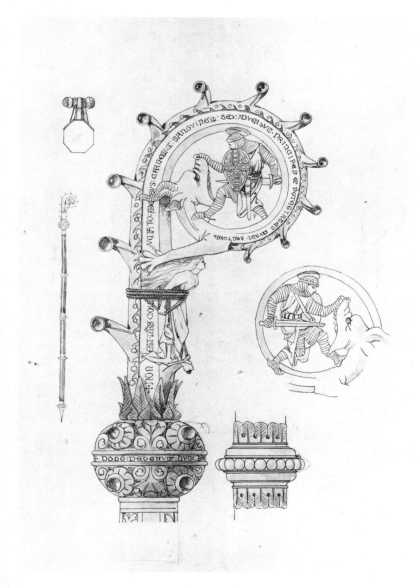

The style of Gothic architecture urged by A.W.N. Pugin in *Contrasts...* (1836) was that of fourteenth century England. This dogma was accepted by his adherents until about 1850 when the need for more flexible Gothic forms became apparent. Partly this was because Gothic was now used for buildings other than churches, which often had no precedents in medieval architecture. There was, too, the need to evolve an economical Gothic style suited to brick architecture and to iron-framed structures. A general freeing of Gothic was marked by William Butterfield's All Saints Church, Margaret Street, London, 1849-50, designed in a highly personal, polychromatic brick style. Ruskin's *Stones of Venice* (1851) praised the merits of Venetian Gothic and the competition of 1855 for a new cathedral at Lille in northern France where the use of brick and an Early French Gothic style were recommended to competitors was won by William Burges (jointly with Henry Clutton). This did much to encourage British architects to study foreign Gothic styles. In 1857, G.G. Scott published *Remarks on Secular & Domestic Architecture* and made a plea for the appropriateness and adaptability of the Gothic style for non-church architecture. These were all landmarks that led, from about 1860, to Gothic's victory in the 'Battle of the Styles' and to an almost universal acceptance that embraced even warehouses, offices and other buildings of commerce. True, Sir George Gilbert Scott lost his campaign for a Gothic Foreign Office but the war might be said to have been won when all the competitors for the Law Courts Competition in 1866 submitted Gothic designs.

Scott's rejected Gothic design for the Foreign Office (1859) was in a French fifteenth century Gothic style (the staircase towers inspired by that at the Chateau de Blois) with a 'squareness and horizontality of outline', and some details, derived from Italian Gothic. For the St Pancras Railway Station and Hotel (1865-76) Scott used a north Italian Gothic 'interlaced with good reproductions of details for Winchester and Salisbury Cathedrals, Westminster Abbey, etc' Burges's church at Studley Royal, Yorkshire (1871-8) was mostly in the Early English Gothic style and so was J.L. Pearson's St Augustine's, London (1870-80). But while the Studley Royal church was a feretory of rich ornament, St Augustine's was the first of a series of vast, chastely decorated churches.

Design for a crozier for the Bishop of Dunedin by William Burges

53 Sir George Gilbert Scott (1811-1878)
Revised design in Gothic style for the Foreign
Office, Whitehall, London, 1859
Perspective of the courtyard side of the Foreign
Office
Pencil, pen, blue pen & watercolour (29 × 53⅜)
(735 × 1285)
Provenance: presented by C.M.O. Scott (architect
grandson of Sir George Gilbert Scott) in 1933

G. G. Scott was a dedicated Gothic Revivalist and
in 1856 when public competitions were
announced for new Foreign and War Offices,
despite rumours that only Classical designs
would be favoured, Scott's entries were in a style
that he described as French Gothic with 'a few
hints from Italy'. In the summer of 1857 the
results of the competitions were announced and
Scott found that he had been awarded the third
premium in the Foreign Office scheme. In the
event, however, the winning designs were
rejected by the Prime Minister, Lord Palmerston.
When his Government fell in February 1858, the

Tories under Lord Derby set up a committee
who eventually appointed Scott as architect for
the new Foreign Office.

The design (a perspective of which is shown
here) followed the general plan and Gothic style
of the competition design and aroused
tremendous controversy within Parliament, the
architectural profession and among the general
public. This 'Battle of the Styles' took an
unexpected turn in May 1859 when the Tory
Government fell and Scott's 'arch-opponent
became once more the autocrat of England'. The
Whigs were determined on a Classical design and
though Scott argued strongly, he eventually
compromised and produced (with M. D. Wyatt) a
Byzanto-Italian design. Lord Palmerston, not
unfairly, regarded it as 'neither one thing nor
other – a regular mongrel affair', and insisted on
a properly Italianate design or resignation. Scott
'bought some costly books on Italian architecture
and set vigorously to work' and the resulting
design was approved by Palmerston and voted
for by Parliament in 1861. Scott's silent protest to

this decision was a medievalizing re-design of the
accepted scheme that he exhibited at the Royal
Academy in 1864 and thus did he square his
Gothic conscience.

Lit: G. Fisher, G. Stamp & others, *The Scott Family,
Catalogue of the Drawings Collection of The Royal
Institute of British Architects*, Amersham, 1981, pp.
53-9

54 John Loughborough Pearson (1817-1897)
Design for the church of St Augustine, Kilburn,
London, *c.* 1874
Interior perspective
Sepia pen & watercolour (37¼ × 21⅞) (945 × 555)
Provenance: purchased in 1931

Best known as a church architect, Pearson's
design for St Augustine's in Kilburn (a poor
parish in north-west London) shows him at his
most masterly. Pevsner has described it as 'one of
the best churches of its date in the whole of
England, a proud, honest, upright achievement'.

Construction of the stone-dressed, brick
church (red brick on the outside, yellow London
stock on the inside) began in 1871 and was
completed, except for the steeple (1897-8), in
1880. The plan is cruciform though from the
nave the transepts are scarcely visible, since the
system of internal buttresses and galleries runs
uninterrupted through the crossing to the
chancel, an idea borrowed from Albi Cathedral
in southern France, though the style, generally, is
Early English.

The perspective shown here was exhibited in
the Architecture Room of the Royal Academy in
1874. One critic, while allowing that it was one of
the best designs exhibited, remarked that 'the
perspective is too sharp and sudden, and
includes too great an angle' (*Builder*, XXXII, 1874,
p. 386). But in fact when checked from the spot
from where, in the imagination, it was drawn, the
drawing is very accurate and the only license
taken is that the bridge is over-acutely angled.
The view was taken from the south-west corner
of the south transept looking into the Lady
Chapel that runs parallel, and with a glimpse
through the crossing into the choir.

Lit: P. Howell, *Victorian Churches*, London, 1968,
pp. 29-30; A. Quiney, *John Loughborough Pearson*,
New Haven and London, 1979, pp. 105-115
et passim.

see Plate X

55 Sir George Gilbert Scott (1811-1878)
Design for St Pancras Railway Station and
Midland Grand Hotel, Euston Road, London,
c. 1865
South elevation, drawn to a scale of 1/10 inch to 1
foot
Pen with sepia pen & wash (29⅛ × 53⅜)
(740 × 1355)
Provenance: presented by C.M.O. Scott (architect
grandson of Sir Geoge Gilbert Scott) in 1953

Scott's entry in a competition (limited to eight
invited architects) for the Midland Railway
Terminus was awarded the first premium in
January, 1866, in spite of the fact that he had
exceeded the requirements of the brief. But a
compromise was reached and the design shown
here was built with one storey omitted. Despite
this and other economies by the time the hotel
was opened in 1873 the cost was approaching
one million pounds. This did include though,
the gigantic iron and glass train shed (43 feet by
690 feet) built in 1866-8 to the design of the
engineers W.H. Barlow and R. M. Ordish.
   The hotel (finally completed in 1876) was the
most splendid in London and, moreover, 'one of
the largest High Victorian Gothic structures in
the world'. The report published in the *Builder*,
1866, that Scott re-used his rejected design for
the Government Offices competition was quite
untrue. Though both designs made use of
French and Italian Gothic details, the massing
and materials are different. Built of red patent
brick, with stone dressings and polished grey and
red granite shafts, the station building and hotel
still stand, though the hotel, alas, is no longer
used as such.

Lit: H. – R. Hitchcock, *Architecture: Nineteenth and
Twentieth Centuries*, Harmondsworth, 1963, pp.
188-9; G. Fisher, G. Stamp & others, *The Scott
Family*, Catalogue of the Drawings Collection of *The
Royal Institute of British Architects*, Amersham, 1981,
pp. 60-1

56 William Burges (1827-1881)
Design for the church of St Mary, Aldford-cum-Studley, near Studley Royal, Yorkshire, *c.* 1872
Interior perspective showing the east end, drawn by Axel Haig (1835-1921)
Watercolour (17 × 13¼) (430 × 340)
Provenance: not known

An outstanding architect-designer, William Burges believed in the Gothic style of the 13th century and his relish for lavish ornament, glittering effects, rich materials and complex iconography were fully realised in his design for St Mary's church at Aldford-cum-Studley. The church, with another also designed by Burges, was built as a memorial to Frederick Grantham Vyner, who, kidnapped by Greek bandits in 1870, was killed in a rescue attempt. The unused ransom money provided some of the funds for the building works.

Built of locally-quarried limestone, St Mary's has a short nave, deep square-ended chancel and at the west end, a tower with spire and pinnacles. Entered from the west door, colour and decoration intensify until the sanctuary with its shallow dome, lace-like vaulting and double-traceried windows, is reached. Marble of different colours, Egyptian alabaster, mosaic, porphyry, frescoes, sculpture and stained glass contribute to an impression of lapidary richness. Iconographically the theme is of 'Paradise Lost and Paradise Regained'. Stylistically, the church is in the Early English style with some Early French influences. It has been justly described as Burges's ecclesiastical masterpiece.

Axel Haig was Burges's favourite perspective artist. He came from Sweden, trained as an architect, turned to architectural perspectives and became also an outstanding etcher.

Lit: J. Mordaunt Crook, *William Burges and the High Victorian Dream*, London, 1981, pp. 229-37

Domestic – all sorts, 1850s-1870s

The country house boom during the middle years of Queen Victoria's reign was created by the growth of industry and commerce. There was a steady increase in home building by the new merchant and manufacturing classes, which started in the early 1850s and reached its peak in the 1870s. This was brought to an abrupt end by the agricultural slump of 1879-94, after which the rich either built much smaller houses or rented them.

'In what style or architecture shall you build your house?', was a common question put to a client during these years, and the relative popularity of different styles became the ever-engrossing topic of Victorian architectural books and journals, competitions or exhibitions at the Royal Academy. Robert Kerr in *The Gentleman's House* (1864) notes that the bewildered gentleman had eleven possible styles to choose from.

Although there was this freedom of choice between styles, their degree of popularity was constantly shifting. Mark Girouard has shown, for example, in *The Victorian Country House*, that the different varieties of Classical styles were losing ground during the mid-Victorian period. Out of a sample of 500 Victorian country houses, 41 per cent were Classical in 1840-4, 32 per cent in 1850-4 and 16 per cent in 1860-4. This was because, since Pugin's writings in the 1830s, Classical architecture had come to be considered un-English and essentially urban – and pagan. (Consequently town-houses remained in a Classical style, or, as in the example of Matthew Digby Wyatt's Alford House, in smart, Parisian Second Empire, a style first copied in the 1850s and used widely for hotels in the 1860s.) For country houses, however, Elizabethan, 'Jacobethan' and Gothic – either English, French or Italian – were acceptable and very commonly used. Antony Salvin and William Burn were at this time the most prolific designers of Elizabethan or baronial mansions; in the Gothic camp the most notable were S.S. Teulon, William Butterfield, William Burges, Benjamin Ferrey and P.C. Hardwick. The latter followed Pugin's design philosophy – that the outside of the house should express what was going on inside, a moralizing system which produced many eccentric and 'muscular' designs. Roumieu's design for a suburban villa at Bushey Heath echoes the stylistic fashion of its grander Gothic prototype.

In the 1860s a number of the younger and abler Gothic Revival architects, and notably W.E. Nesfield and R. Norman Shaw, inaugurated the 'Old English' style, which was a term used to describe both Tudor Gothic and Elizabethan of the rambling, manorial kind. Shaw's design for Leyswood was particularly influential. In so doing they declared their distaste for the modern Gothic of plate-glass sash-windows and structural polychromy, and led the way to the Arts & Crafts Movement, which turned its attention to the vernacular tradition of humble country dwellings, and to ways of building rather than stylistic correctness.

Sketch design for the turret, staircase and coachman's rooms at Ampton Hall, Suffolk, *c.* 1848, by S.S. Teulon

57 Philip Brown (working *c.* 1852-1854)
Design for Brownsea Castle, Brownsea Island,
Dorset, for Colonel William Petrie Waugh,
c. 1852
Perspective
Watercolour (29½ × 52) (750 × 1320)
Provenance: purchased in 1976

This large and painterly perspective, very much
in the spirit of Joseph Nash's *Mansions of England
in the Olden Time*, must have well suited the
pretensions of its nouveau-riche client. Colonel
Waugh bought Brownsea Island in 1852 in the
belief that it possessed resources of china clay,
valued at about one million pounds sterling. In
view of the certainty of an enormous sum, the
unsophisticated Colonel began rebuilding the
castle, which dated back as an island fortress to
the time of Henry VIII. Philip Brown, an
unknown architect from Southampton, lavishly
echoed this Tudor past with a haze of
battlements, turrets and castellated jetties.

It is likely that Brown's design was executed in
a modified form, although it is difficult to
estimate the extent of the building works as the
castle was gutted by fire in 1896 and partly
rebuilt at the beginning of this century. It is still
castellated but with fewer turrets; the jetty exists
in a modified form as does the clock tower on the
right. Brown also designed the nearby church of
St Mary in 1854.

By 1870, however, Colonel Waugh and his
company, the Branksea Clay and Pottery
Company, had gone bankrupt as the geological
experts were proved wrong.

Lit: *Country Life*, XLIX, 1921, pp. 430-6;
J. Newman and N. Pevsner, *Dorset*, London, 1973,
pp 117-18; J. Physick and M. Darby, *Marble Halls*,
catalogue of an exhibition, London 1973, no. 21;
G. Stamp, *The Great Perspectivists*, London,
1982, p.51

see Plate XI

58 Robert Louis Roumieu (1814-1877)
Design for a house at Bushey Heath,
Hertfordshire, for Owen T. Alger, *c.* 1855
Perspective
Pen & watercolour on paper watermarked 1855
(18½ × 24) (48 × 61)
Provenance: presented by J. Fox Jones in 1956

Roumieu was, to use Goodhart-Rendel's term, a
'rogue architect' of the High Victorian period.
He was in partnership with A. D. Gough from
1836-1848 and with him built Milner Square in
Islington in the 1840s and many other churches,
schools, commercial and domestic buildings.
Their work is full of wild fantasies and their
drawings form the most colourful group in the

Collection. These present an alternative
architecture, not of the artistic or tasteful kind,
but reflecting the healthy preoccupations of the
suburban nouveau-riche.

It is not known if this design for a suburban
villa at Bushey Heath was ever carried out, but it
was the final design: alternative schemes exist in
an Italianate style. Possibly this Tudor design
with Gothic additions was considered more up to
date: certainly it is an amazing amalgam of the
architectural ideas of the 1850s.

An earlier Tudor house is to be remodelled.
Smart modern conservatories are clapped on the
east and west sides, and Gothic dormers of the
Picturesque kind, deriving from Loudon's
Encyclopaedia, are punched into the roof above

tile-capped bays: this is the hard Gothic of plate
glass windows much hated by the architects of
the later Arts & Crafts Movement. The central
octagonal bay, embedded in the centre of the
facade, is fantastic and original. The lower storey
is contemporary 'muscular' Gothic breaking into
an open timber balcony surmounted by a conical
roof. It has echoes of S.S. Teulon and of Gothic
buildings in Normandy.

Lit: H. S. Goodhart-Rendel, 'Rogue architects of
the Victorian Era', *RIBA Journal*, LVI, 1949, p.
255; J. Physick and M. Darby, '*Marble Halls*,
catalogue of an exhibition, London, 1973, no. 22.

59 Richard Norman Shaw (1831-1912)
Design for Leyswood, Groombridge, Sussex, for
James William Temple, 1868
Bird's-eye perspective
Pen (22½ × 33) (575 × 840)
Provenance: presented by Mrs Norman Shaw in
1916

Shaw made his debut at the Royal Academy in
1870 with two perspectives of Leyswood, a low-
level view and the bird's-eye view shown here.
The invention of photolithography enabled them
to be published in the architectural press, and
consequently the design for Leyswood strongly
influenced domestic architecture both in Britain
and in the United States, where it inspired the
first essays in the 'Shingle style'.

The 'Old English' of Leyswood was radically
different from the standard Gothic country
house style of the 1860s. The impression given is
of Tudor half-timbered fragments and towers,
with great 17th century chimneys, linked by
rustic vernacular ranges. The *Builder* disapproved
of this vernacular element saying that it was a
'revival of the past which it is more lawful to
indulge in in a private country house for the
gratifying of a man's own taste, than in more
public places.'

Shaw's draughtsmanship made an impact on
architects for its cold, literal qualities; the
drawings were clear and easy to copy. They were
not, however, very captivating for they were
ruled in black pen, without washes or shadows,
(the pupils in his office used a jagged T-square to
rule in the tiling and brickwork) and the
landscape surroundings were uninviting. It is
known, however, that Shaw did not want to
produce picturesque watercolour perspectives
for he regretted the popularising efforts of
architects in the Royal Academy Architecture
Room. He wanted to return to the old style of
elevation 'with, of course, the well-dressed ladies
and gentlemen and the hansom cabs...carefully
omitted'.

Today, only the stable wing (left) of Leyswood
still stands.

Lit: *Builder*, XXVIII, 1870, p. 359; A.
Saint, *Richard Norman Shaw*, New Haven and
London, 1976, fig. 25 *et passim*; G. Stamp, *The
Great Perspectivists*, London, 1982, no. 77

60 Sir Matthew Digby Wyatt (1820-1877)
Design for Alford House, Princes Gate, London,
for Lady Marion Alford, 1872
Perspective
Sepia pen & wash (23½ × 39¾) (600 × 1010)
Provenance: purchased in 1979

Alford House was the most elegant 'Second
Empire' mansion in London and stood in
Princes Gate at the corner of Ennismore Gardens
until it was demolished in 1955.

The influence of the French Second Empire
style had come to England after the English had
swarmed to Paris to visit the International
Exhibition of 1855 and had seen L.T.J. Visconti's
and H.M. Lefuel's New Louvre. In the
competition of 1856-7 for a new Foreign Office
and War Office, the prizewinners were in the
pavilioned and mansarded manner, deriving as
much from the Tuileries as from the New
Louvre. The winning designs of Garling and Coe
were extensively illustrated in the journals and
were favourite stylistic models in the 1860s –
particularly becoming the accepted style for the
hotel boom in that decade and for the mansions
of the wealthy.

Wyatt himself was very much a new European
and served as juror on furniture and decoration
at the Paris International Exhibition of 1855. He
was much noted for his 'effective and powerful'
perspectives and this one drew a lengthy
comment in the *Builder* when it was exhibited in
1872. His draughtsmanship was praised but not
the decorative aspects of the building. The *Builder*
regretted 'the array of great carved festoons
under the cornice; what, let us seriously ask, is
the gain to the building for the time and expense
that must have been bestowed in carving this
used-up ornamental feature all round?' This was
the view of a magazine still strongly committed
to the moralizing theories of the Gothic Revival
and opposed to the introduction of a foreign
style.

Lit: *Builder*, XXX, 1872, p. 358; H. – R.
Hitchcock, *Architecture: Nineteenth and Twentieth
Centuries*, Harmondsworth, 1958, ch. 9

61 George Aitchison (1825-1910)
Design for the interior of 1 Grosvenor Crescent,
Belgravia, London, for Sir Wilfrid Lawson,
c. 1887
Part-elevation, part-section of the staircase well
Watercolour (38 × 20) (965 × 510)
Provenance: presented to the RIBA by George
Aitchison's executors in 1910

Aitchison's decorative style for this interior – now
unfortunately destroyed although the house itself
still stands – is close to the 'aesthetic' interior of
the 1870s, the style associated with Whistler's
Peacock Room of 1877 and Linley Sambourne's
18 Stafford Terrace. They too used ebonized
woodwork, dados and floral papers.

The woodwork in this house was inlaid with
ivory, mother-of-pearl and lapis lazuli, and the
floral sprays and panels of flying birds were
designed by Aitchison but hand-painted,
possibly by the artist Frederick Smallfield, who
had worked for Aitchison on Mr Lehman's house
at 15 Berkeley Square. What distinguishes
Aitchison's design from the dull 'aesthetic'
colours in vogue in the 1870s is the opulence of
the colour schemes: two other designs for this
house in the Collection show that the hall was a
rich olive green and the drawing room bright
yellow, both with ebony woodwork.

Aitchison, who was an architect and
distinguished man in the profession, is best
known for his fashionable decorative work and
was without doubt the most exhibited decorator
for three decades. His Royal Academy drawings
(the best of which are preserved at the RIBA) are
some of the most exquisite of the 19th century
and were praised as such in their own day. His
finest work was the house he designed and
decorated throughout for Lord Leighton in
Holland Park Road, Kensington. The Arab Hall,
particularly, which he added to the house in
1877 to display Leighton's collection of Saracenic
tiles, established him as a master of decoration
and ornament and led to a large number of
commissions from influential clients, many in
artistic circles though Sir Wilfrid Lawson was a
politician and temperance advocate.

Aitchison's significance lies chiefly in his
patronage of decorative painting and craft by
other artists, but with the exception of the Arab
Hall, his interiors have all disappeared and can
only be judged by his drawings at the RIBA.

Lit: M. Richardson 'George Aitchison: Lord
Leighton's architect', *RIBA Journal* LXXX, 1980,
no 1, pp. 37-40

see Plate XII

Eclecticism, 1870s-1880s

As we have seen, the mid-Victorian decades were dominated by the Gothic Revival architects. Sir George Gilbert Scott was the most prolific and the buildings that stand out as the monuments of that style are Scott's St Pancras Station Hotel, Alfred Waterhouse's Manchester Town Hall and G.E. Street's Law Courts.

But in the 1860s many architects, and particularly the young and progressive among them, like Nesfield and Shaw, began to turn away from Gothic forms – especially in their domestic work – towards Old English and the Queen Anne style. The latter, with its Flemish counterpart, was developed by Ernest George and Harold Peto in London for their houses in Harrington Gardens in the 1880s, and then copied all over Chelsea.

Gothic itself had since the 1850s taken many forms; Ruskin had made the north Italian Gothic of Venice and Verona respectable. After this it was only a small step to total eclecticism and after about 1860 most architects felt free to choose and to vary their choice and combination of styles from building to building.

The styles displayed by the group of buildings in South Kensington called 'Albertopolis', after Prince Albert, the main sponsor of the Great Exhibition of 1851, well illustrate the eclecticism of the period. In 1859 work was begun on the first buildings of the Victoria and Albert Musuem. These were designed by Captain Francis Fowke in an Italian Renaissance style derived from the north of Italy. Next came the Albert Memorial of 1862 by Sir Gilbert Scott in an Italian Gothic, to be followed by Lt-Colonel H.Y.D. Scott's Albert Hall of 1867, which was modelled on the Classical German of the Dresden Opera House of 1837-41. Waterhouse's preference was for German Romanesque for the Natural History Museum, 1873, and the last major public building in Albertopolis – the Imperial Institute of 1887-93 – was in the style of the French Early Renaissance, inspired by the châteaux of the Loire.

Sketch of the Giralda Tower, Seville, Spain by Andrew Noble Prentice (1866-1941), 1889

62 Alfred Waterhouse (1830-1905)
Designs for interior galleries in the Natural
History Museum, London, 1870-71:
a. Perspective of the 'skeleton' gallery
Pen & sepia wash on tracing paper (10¾ × 12¾)
(275 × 325)
b. Perspective of the 'monkey arch'
Pen & sepia wash on tracing paper (10½ × 15¼)
(265 × 400)
Provenance: presented by Michael Waterhouse
(the architect's grandson) and Cedric Ripley in
1933

These two drawings are for interiors in
Waterhouse's preliminary design of 1870-71;
signed, they are in his own characteristically
delicate and lively hand.

Waterhouse had been called in to revise
Captain Fowke's winning competition design
after the latter's death in 1865; he reworked the
plans in 1870-71 and converted Fowke's
Renaissance facades into German Romanesque.
This change was partly due to the wish of the
museum's director, Sir Richard Owen, to have
the building decorated with figures of plants and
animals symbolic of its contents; lavish
decoration with birds and beasts of all kinds was
a feature of Romanesque but not of Renaissance
architecture. The internal and external
decoration of the museum provides one of the
great pleasures in walking around the building;
Waterhouse himself believed that it was the task
of the architect 'to clothe over practical
necessities with such beauty as they were capable
of receiving'. It was the first building in England
where the main facades were entirely faced with
terracotta, a material which was chosen because
it produced cheap durable ornament from
moulds. It could also be washed at regular
intervals, and was last cleaned in 1975, with
breathtaking results.

The ornament was divided into two main
classes; the west or zoological half was decorated
with living specimens, the east, geological half
with extinct ones. Inside, too, the terracotta
decoration was carefully designed to supplement
the teaching of the exhibits, as can be seen in this
design for the 'monkey arch'. Waterhouse
himself made the drawings for the reliefs, on the
basis of material supplied by Owen; the
terracotta was then cast from models made by M.
Dujardin, who worked for Farmer and Brindley

the architectural modellers. The design for the
'skeleton' gallery shows how Waterhouse
deliberately displayed the iron and concrete
structure, although he clad it in plaster and
terracotta decoration. Daylighting came from the
lower slopes of the roof rather than from directly
overhead, the arrangement generally regarded as
the best one at the time, although these ideas
were superseded when electricity was introduced
between 1900 and 1914. Similarly most of the
original exhibition cases seen here, which were
designed by Waterhouse or Sir John Taylor,
surveyor to the Office of Works, have been
dismantled. The Museum was built from
1873-81, to modified designs.

Lit: *Survey of London*, The Museums Area of South
Kensington and Westminster, XXXVIII, London,
1975; M. Girouard, *Alfred Waterhouse and the
Natural History Museum*, New Haven and London,
1981

63 Sir Ernest George (1839-1922) and Harold
Ainsworth Peto (1854-1933)
Design for 50 and 52 Cadogan Square, Chelsea,
London, for Colonel Thynne and Thomas
Andros De La Rue, 1885
Perspective, dated 1885 on the gable
Sepia pen & wash (25¾ × 19¼) (655 × 485)
Provenance: presented by Alfred B. Yeates in
1935

The Queen Anne style had emerged as a
coherent manner of building in the late 1860s as
a direct reaction against the widespread
commercialism of Gothic. The Flemish style
grew out of Queen Anne, inspired by the
example set by Norman Shaw's 196 Queens Gate·
which set the fashion in 1874. The architect,
however, who made the style his own was Ernest
George. In his houses in Collingham and
Harrington Gardens, Kensington, of 1881-84, he
produced a series of highly picturesque Flemish
burghers' houses which became very fashionable
patterns in the 1880s, particularly in Chelsea and
Kensington.

This design for two houses in Cadogan Square
shows the two styles most commonly used by
George and Peto. The larger house on the left,
No 52, for Thomas Andros De La Rue, the
printer of stamps and playing cards, is in the
Flemish style, with applied Renaissance and
Jacobean detailing and an elaborately shaped
brick gable. Colonel Thynne's house is in a
plainer Queen Anne, with a central canted bay
window and shutters for the upper floors. Both
are built in brick, as was specified by the
Cadogan and Hans Place Estate Company, but
the De La Rue house has terracotta dressings
made by Doulton's. The two designs were meant
to complement each other, each offering as
many picturesque features as possible; the
'quaintly shaped' bay window forming the
entrance porch in No. 52 was seen at the time to
be particularly interesting.

This perspective is a good example of Ernest
George's soft, sepia pen and wash technique
which was well suited to conveying the textures
of natural materials and the picturesque effects
of random street architecture.

The *Builder* was not particularly impressed by
the design when it was exhibited at the Royal
Academy in 1886 and wrote: 'A picturesque
brown-tinted drawing showing houses decorated
with flat scroll ornaments in brickwork, and
rusticated pilasters standing on corbels, and with
no meaning or architectural function of any
kind. But this is the fashion now, and the authors
cater for it better than most of their
contemporaries... No plan.'

Lit: *Builder*, L, 1886, pp 708, 710-11;
M. Girouard, *Sweetness and Light*, Oxford, 1977,
passim.

64 Arthur Beresford Pite (1861-1934)
Competition design for a 'West-End Club
House' for the Soane Medallion Prize, 1882
Perspective, with presentation plans attached
(added after the competition)
Pen (36 × 25 & 4¼ × 25) (915 × 635 & 110 × 635)
Provenance: presented by Ian Pite in 1937

Beresford Pite won the RIBA's Soane Medallion
Prize with this spectacular drawing when he was
twenty-one and still a junior assistant in John
Belcher's office.

The Pite family was full of architects: Beresford
was first articled to his father's firm before
joining Belcher, and at the same time took a
course in drawing from William Richardson at
the Royal College of Art, developing a lasting
interest in Dürer's techniques. His drawing
shows the influences of Dürer, William Burges
and the extraordinary mediaeval fantasies of
H.W. Brewer, who regularly produced
illustrations for the *Builder*.

Pite's bravura draughtsmanship was highly
personal in style. It is always possible to
recognise the thick agitated line and hatched
skies of a Pite drawing: Goodhart-Rendel once
said that his clouds always looked like 'pillow
cases caught up in telegraph wires'. John
Betjemen characterised the style of this design as
'Wagnerian Romantic' and noted that Pite had
also designed the West End to go with his club
house. His pseudonym for the competition was
El Dorado/Yo hé trovado.

Pite later had a successful career. The least
predictable of architects, he produced buildings
in many different styles. His best-known works
are 82, Mortimer Street, London, 1896 in a
Michelangelesque-revival style, and the free-
Byzantine Christ Church, Brixton Road,
London, 1897-8.

Lit: *Building News*, XLII, 1882, p. 386; *Builder*,
XLII, 1882, p. 279; J. Betjeman, *First and Last
Loves*, London, 1952, p. 175; A. Service, 'Arthur
Beresford Pite', *Edwardian Architecture and its
Origins*, London, 1975, pp 394-404; G. Stamp,
The Great Perspectivists, London, 1982, no 112

65 Thomas Edward Collcutt (1840-1924)
Contract design for the Principal Tower of the
Imperial Institute, South Kensington, London,
8th August, 1888
South elevation and section, with plans at various
levels, and details, with the signatures of the
contractors, John Mowlem Burt, W. R. Freeman,
and George Burt Jr.
Pen & with coloured washes (28½ × 21)
(725 × 535)
Provenance: presented by Stanley Hamp of
Collcutt and Hamp in 1955

To commemorate Queen Victoria's Jubilee the
Prince of Wales had, in the summer of 1886, the
idea of perpetuating the Colonial Exhibition in
permanent form as the Imperial Institute. It was
to be both a museum and exhibition centre,
dealing with all things concerning India and the
colonies – its intention being to encourage
emigration, expand trade and symbolise the
Empire. The site chosen was one just south of
the Royal Albert Hall, which pleased Queen
Victoria as realising Prince Albert's ideas for a
cultural centre in South Kensington.

A limited competition was held in 1887 and
the architects chosen to compete were Aston
Webb and E. Ingress Bell, T.G. Jackson, A.W.
Blomfield, R. Rowand Anderson, T.N. Deane &
Son and Collcutt. Alfred Waterhouse was the
architectural assessor. Collcutt's scheme was
chosen: the assessors particularly liked his simple
symmetrical plan, good silhouette and the
binding horizontal strips and courses. Jackson
recalls that Waterhouse told him that when his
design was unpacked he had said, 'Oh that's the
one' but that his planning was inferior. Jackson's
design had looked like a college with a huge
Flemish tower, whereas Collcutt's was French
Early Renaissance in style with motifs borrowed
from Chambord.

The tower rose to a height of 287 feet, with a
copper dome, and housed a peal of ten bells
donated by an Australian lady. The drawing
shows Collcutt's idiosyncratic use of materials:
brick is laid in fine thin strips as if it were more
precious than Portland stone.

The Institute was formally opened on 10th
May 1893 by Queen Victoria, but sadly failed to
find a permanent role for itself in the 20th
century. Its demolition from 1957-1965, to make
way for Imperial College, provoked vigorous
agitation from the general public. These
objections led not only to the retention of the
Tower but to the formation of the Victorian
Society in 1958.

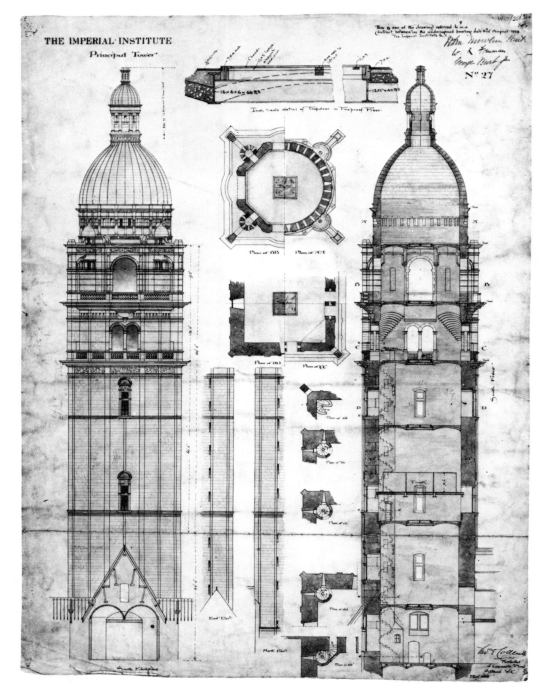

Lit: B.H. Jackson, *Recollections of Thomas Graham
Jackson 1835-1924,* London, 1950, p.210;
J. Physick and M. Darby, *Marble Halls,* catalogue
of an exhibition, 1973, no. 141

The Arts and Crafts Movement

Design for a metal hinge by C.F.A. Voysey, 1896, from Volume II, Quarto Imperial Club volumes

The precursors of the Arts and Crafts Movement were George Devey, Philip Webb, the architect of William Morris's Red House, and William E. Nesfield and R. Norman Shaw. Devey was the first Victorian architect to design new buildings based on a local 'vernacular' style, at Penshurst in Kent in as early as 1850; Shaw and Nesfield sketched humble rural buildings in Yorkshire and Kent in 1861-2, and as we have seen, launched the 'Old English' style with the design for Leyswood in 1868.

During the 1880s and 90s the younger, more progressive architects, many of them in Shaw's office, tried to free their work from historical styles, and instead based their designs on the examples of simple, country buildings – on the 'vernacular'. They followed a new pursuit, 'scrambling': energetically travelling through the villages of Kent, Surrey and Sussex sketching local utilitarian buildings. Most of them joined the new guilds and societies: the two most important of these were the Society for the Protection of Ancient Buildings (SPAB), founded by William Morris in 1877 and presided over by Philip Webb, and the Art Workers' Guild, started in 1884 by five pupils in Shaw's office, Gerald Horsley, W. R. Lethaby, Ernest Newton, Mervyn Macartney and Edward Prior. The Society was founded specifically to prevent the ruthless Gothic 'restoration' of cathedrals and other ancient monuments, and was a strong force in making younger architects aware of the materials and textures of traditional building and the value of craftsmanship. The aim of the Art Workers' Guild was to bring together craftsmen in architecture, painting, sculpture and the applied arts, and its architect members particularly wanted to bring craft and the arts back again into

building. The architects of the Movement, and their buildings, came to be called 'Arts and Crafts' after the name given in 1888 to the Arts and Crafts Exhibition Society (an offshoot of the Art Workers' Guild). Their work has certain common features: the functions of a building were expressed in its exterior form; its materials were taken from the immediate locality as being cheaper and in harmony with its surroundings. Details were based on vernacular originals and not taken from classical pattern books. They were all interested in craft and in employing plasterers, painters, carvers and sculptors to enrich their work; ornament was based on Nature.

Although these features were common to the Movement, there were as well many variations and inconsistencies in theory and in ways of building. There were those who concentrated on the 'essentials', like C.F.A. Voysey, E.S. Prior and W.R. Lethaby; others who were more interested in elaborate craft than in building, like Gerald Horsley. There were the church architects like J.D. Sedding, Temple Moore and Ninian Comper who chose to develop a modern crafted Gothic based not on French prototypes but on English Perpendicular, and those who turned to Byzantine for anti-Gothic reasons, like Beresford Pite, J.F. Bentley and Henry Wilson. Some, like Halsey Ricardo, wanted colourful washable surfaces to buildings, and different again were those who based their work on late seventeenth century vernacular Classicism, like Ernest Newton. There was also the 'artiness' of Baillie Scott, the progressiveness of the Scottish architect C.R. Mackintosh and the picturesque romanticism of Edwin Lutyens: the three most influential architects of the Movement.

66 Sir Edwin Lutyens (1869-1944)
Preliminary design for additions to the Ferry Inn
at Rosneath,Dumbartonshire, Scotland, for
H.R.H. Princess Louise, Duchess of Argyll, 1896
South & east elevations & rough perspective
sketch, to a scale of 1/10 inch to 1 foot
Pen & watercolour with pencil additions
(17 × 27½) (430 × 700)
Provenance: presented by Robert Lutyens,
(Lutyens's son) in 1951

In 1896 H.R.H. Princess Louise, daughter of
Queen Victoria and wife of the Marquess of
Lorne, commissioned additions to the Ferry Inn
on the shores of Gareloch. Lutyens, then aged
twenty-seven, was obviously anxious to make his
mark, for he rarely added watercolour to his
design sketches; the design is also interesting as
being his earliest essay in the classical style.

The new wing, to contain reception rooms and
a bar with bedrooms above, is added to an

existing Scottish building, shown on the left of
each elevation. Lutyens, no doubt to impress his
client, has incorporated several inappropriately
grand features – for example the elaborate
Baroque front door with segmental pediment
and the mannered east elevation with its semi-
circular widows. Typical of Lutyens, however, is
the way the Inn is built into the slope of the
hillside, the batter of the lower walls and the
exaggerated manner of curving out the foot of
the tiled roof. The scheme was abandoned later
for one that incorporated many more local
features; the original Inn was demolished in
1960 and the truncated remains of the Lutyens
wing are all that now remain.

Lutyens first met Princess Louise through
Gertrude Jekyll, the landscape gardener, for
whom he designed Munstead Wood in 1895-6.
The Princess, who was a talented craftswoman
and sculptor, took up the young architect, who
was not unnaturally flattered by frequent

summonses to Kensington Palace. He found the
Princess difficult to resist, 'one makes believe and
has jokes innumerable', and pointed out to Lady
Emily, his future wife, the prestige value of the
connection, for the Princess's Mama might want
to rebuild Windsor Castle.

Lit: C. Hussey, *The Life of Sir Edwin Lutyens*,
London, 1950, pp. 56,71-2, 146; M. Richardson,
*Edwin Lutyens, Catalogue of the Drawings Collection of
the Royal Institute of British Architiects*, Farnborough,
1973, [252]. p. 45; *Lutyens*, Arts Council catalogue
of an exhibition, London 1981, pp. 80-81

HOVSE FOR JVLIAN · STVRGIS · ESQ.re AT PVTTENHAM NEAR GVILDFORD · SVRREY

67 Charles Francis Annesley Voysey (1857-1941)
Design for Greyfriars, Puttenham, on the Hog's
Back, Surrey, for Julian Sturgis, 1897
Perspective of the garden front, with inset
ground and first floor plans, drawn by H. Gaye
Pencil & watercolour (15¾ × 27½) (400 × 695)
Provenance: presented by Charles Cowles Voysey
in 1941

The Sturgis house, known variously as
'Merlshanger' or 'Wancote' and now called
'Greyfriars' has the simplicity of Voysey's best
houses. It is situated high up on the Hog's Back
looking southwards over Surrey, and is of the
type of long, narrow house Voysey repeated
several times, the rooms lined up in the plan
partly to allow as many as possible to enjoy the
view. The walls are roughcast and the windows
are arranged in long regular strips along the
elevations. A compact rectangular range has a
cross-gable at one end, the roof of which sweeps

right down to eaves below the line of the ground
floor windows.

Voysey produced only about fifty buildings,
most of which were houses or cottages. He was
well illustrated in the architectural press and
consequently highly influential as a designer, but
his practice virtually ceased in 1914. His
reputation revived in the 1930s when he came to
be seen as a 'pioneer' of the Modern Movement.
Hermann Muthesius in his book on the English
house in 1904 had noted Voysey's 'total
abandonment of historical tradition', and that
there was 'an air of primitivism about his
houses'. This primitive, almost naive, simplicity
can especially be seen in his presentation
perspectives which are characterised by the use
of bright clear colours and labelled in a script
designed by Voysey himself.

His inflexibility in dealing with clients
undoubtedly lost him a number of jobs in the
years preceding the First World War. He

expected to have total control not only over the
design of the house but also over the design of its
fittings. As these were specially crafted a Voysey
house could often prove to be very expensive.
He also liked to design the wallpapers, textiles
and furniture; the daughter of one of his clients,
the present owner of White Cottage, Wandsworth,
still has the original plain green curtains that
Voysey specified for all the windows in the
house.

Lit: J. Symonds, *C.F.A. Voysey, Catalogue of the
Drawings Collection of the Royal Institute of British
Architects*, Amersham, 1976, [117]; D. Simpson,
C.F.A. Voysey: an architect of individuality, London
1979, p. 44 fig. 16; G. Stamp, *The Great
Perspectivists*, London,1982, no. 90

119

68 Charles Francis Annesley Voysey (1857-1941)
Design for a wallpaper showing watersnakes
among weed, for Essex & Co., *c.* 1889
Coloured washes (17 × 16⅜) (440 × 420)
Provenance: presented by Charles Cowles Voysey
in 1941

Voysey's early pattern designs for wallpapers and
textiles (from about 1883 to 1893) are
characterised by the use of flowing curves, and
came to have an influence on Continental Art
Nouveau. This particular wallpaper design,
although undated, is related to a similar snake
design in the Victoria and Albert Musuem, dated
1889.

Voysey's work was first shown, and much
admired, at the Paris Exhibition of 1889.
Wallpapers by Jeffrey & Co. and Essex & Co.
were shown at the 'Salon de l'Association pour
l'Art d'Anvers' in 1893, and it was this exhibition
which led to the article by Henry Van de Velde in
L'Art Moderne on 'Artistic Wallpapers'. All the
English papers were admired but Van de Velde
wrote of the Voysey designs as being head and
shoulders above the others. Both Van de Velde
and Victor Horta used Voysey papers in their Art
Nouveau buildings.

It is ironic, however, that Voysey came later
strongly to disapprove of Art Nouveau and all
foreign influences on design, much as he also
disapproved of foreign travel. In 1904 he
referred to Art Nouveau as being 'distinctly
unhealthy and revolting', and from the 1890s his
patterns lose their flowing curves and form
strongly repeating patterns of juxtaposed and
simplified shapes.

From the 1880s right into the 1930s his pattern
designs supported him when building
commissions were scarce; by 1890 he was
designing for Jeffrey's, Woollam's, Sanderson's
and John Line and from 1890 to 1900 he had a
contract to supply the Essex Company with
twenty designs a year. Every Voysey design
incorporated forms that were part of everyday
life or part of the world of legend and fairytale,
which should both affect the imagination and be
immediately comprehensible. He particularly felt
that Nature was 'the great fount of inspiration'
and spoke with disgust of those who were
satisfied with a Persian rug 'without being able to
interpret its symbolism or derive from it one
spark of intellectual life'.

Lit: P. Floud, in *Penrose Annual*, LII, 1858, pp. 10-
14; M. Richardson, 'Wallpapers by C.F.A.
Voysey', *RIBA Journal*, LXXII, 1965, pp. 399-403,
reprd.p. 399; E. Aslin in *C.F.A. Voysey: architect and
designer 1857-1941*, catalogue of an exhibition,
Brighton, 1978, pp. 96-100, fig. D.48

see Plate XIII

69 Ernest Newton (1856-1922)
Design for Fouracre, West Green, Hampshire, *c.* 1902
Perspective of the entrance front, drawn by Thomas Hamilton Crawford
Pencil & watercolour (9¾ × 14½) (250 × 370)
Provenance: presented by Christopher Newton, son of the architect, in 1969

Ernest Newton's work was very influential. He created a manner of design that became standard until the Second World War, of alternating between the Georgian and vernacular styles for country houses, a system much taken up by Lutyens and Guy Dawber in the 1900s, but started by Newton in the early 1890s.

Fouracre is very characteristic of his work. The house, as depicted in this almost fairy-tale perspective by T. Hamilton Crawford, epitomises his unmannered country-Georgian style that gives the impression of a building well rooted in the countryside for a couple of hundred years. It is a house embodying many of the ideals of the Arts & Crafts Movement, of the kind described by the architect W. H. Bidlake in *The Modern Home*: 'There it stands, overgrown with ivy and sheltered by tall trees, in detached seclusion, content to let the busy life pass it by on the distant high road. It speaks of other days, when life moved more leisurely, and when the many inventions which yearly make our modern life more feverish, were unknown.' The design shows Newton's straightforward use of traditional building materials. The house is of red brick, with ornamental diaper bands of red and grey bricks and tiles; it has shuttered sashes to distinguish the reception rooms and lead casements for the remainder. The scale is, however, deceptive, for the house has nine bedrooms.

Lit: W.S. Sparrow, *The Modern Home*, n.d. (reprd. as frontispiece); W.G. Newton, *The Work of Ernest Newton RA*, 1925, pp. 62-68
see Plate XIV

70 Henry Wilson (1864-1934)
Design for the extension of the east end of St
Bartholomew's church, Brighton, Sussex, *c.* 1898
Interior perspective
Charcoal, gouache & watercolours (52¼ × 30¾)
(1335 × 780)
Provenance: presented by the Victoria & Albert
Museum in 1955

Henry Wilson was a pupil of J.D. Sedding, a
leading ecclesiastical architect of the Arts &
Crafts Movement, and took over his practice on
his death in 1891. He had been devoted to
Sedding and shared his beliefs, not only in
uniting craft with building, but that the architect
should be 'the invisible, inspiring, ever active
force animating all the activities necessary for the
production of architecture.'

Wilson's drawings are the most dramatically
presented of the Movement, and the largest. The
draughtsmanship is vigorous, the medium often
charcoal and watercolour or gouache and
coloured chalks, mostly on grey or blue sugar
paper, not white cartridge. The architectural
journals of the time, particularly the *Builder*, were
aware of their novel effect, which generally they
found splendid although 'wanting in architectural
refinement'.

Wilson's sense of drama is best shown in this
scheme for the extension and redecoration of St
Batholomew's, Brighton, a vast brick church
built by Edmund Scott in 1872-4. He intended to
pierce the east wall of the church and turn it into
an openwork screen, and then continue the main
structure for three bays to form a Lady Chapel.
The new east wall was to be covered with a mural
representing the Mother of God in Glory about
30 feet high. The effect is overwhelmingly
Byzantine; all that was carried out however, from
1899-1908, was the baldaccino, the altar and its
fittings, pulpit and giant candlesticks.

Lit: N. Taylor in *Architectural Review CXXXIX,*
1966, pp. 274-277; P. Howell, *Victorian Churches,*
London, 1968, pl. 43

71 Gerald Callcott Horsley (1862-1917)
Design for the interior decoration of the chancel,
Church of All Saints, Leek, Staffordshire, 1891
Interior perspective
Pen & watercolour (27 × 19¾) (685 × 505)
Provenance: presented by Mrs Gerald Horsley in
1918

Gerald Horsley was the son of the Victorian
genre painter, J. C. Horsley, and was trained in
Norman Shaw's office. He had a comparatively
small architectural practice of his own, designing
houses, churches and schools, but his métier was
church decorative work.

He had been one of the original founder
members of the Art Workers' Guild in 1884, and
the general principle underlying the foundation
of the Guild – the attempt to merge the arts of
painting, decoration and carving with architecture
– was a theme often expressed in his writings,
notably in an essay, 'The Union of Art' in
Architecture, a Profession or an Art?, edited by
R. Norman Shaw and T.G. Jackson in 1891.

All Horsley's works are characterised by a love
of carved or painted decoration, and his principal
jobs were for decorative work in churches
designed by Shaw. He was also one of the ablest
draughtsman of his time and was constantly used
by his Arts and Crafts colleagues as a perspective
artist. This perspective shows his typical drawing
style. It is in watercolour with black pen, his
scratchy line marvellously presenting the textures
of different materials. The *Builder* wrote about
the drawing when it was exhibited at the Royal
Academy in 1891: 'The nearer portion of the
chancel wall is occupied by a Gothic-looking
diaper ornament arranged on net-work
lines...near the trunk two angels stand under the
foliage; the whole being treated in a quite flat
and decorative manner. The roof timbers are
painted in a manner based on Mediaeval
examples. The remainder of the decoration is
original in design, and the colour effect of the
drawing has a decided character of its own'. All
Saints, Leek, was a church designed by Shaw in
1885-1887

Lit: *Builder*, LXI, 1891, p. 497; A. Saint, *Richard
Norman Shaw*, New Haven and London, 1976,
passim.

Design for Isotype dwellings by Wells Coates, *c.* 1932

The Twentieth Century

By 1914 a revolution had taken place in architecture: a number of different architects in different countries had succeeded in creating a manner of building that was independent of past styles. Walter Gropius's factory, the Fagus Works at Alfeld in Germany, of 1911-14, has often been cited as the first example of the new International Modern movement, but there are other examples of seminal work: F. Lloyd Wright's houses in the 1890s in Chicago and his 1902 Yahara Boat Club project; Tony Garnier's Cité Industrielle of 1904; the works of Joseph Hoffman and Adolf Loos in Vienna, and Behrens's turbine factory in Berlin of 1909. The buildings of the new style were characterised by their unrelievedly cubic general shapes and were mostly rendered white. They were intended to be built of machine-made materials and to express their function in their form; they avoided references to motifs of the past – period detail, classical columns or pitched roofs. It has been said that the new architecture was distinguished by a 'new sense of space and the machine aesthetic'. In addition, through easier travel, the spread of cheap printing and a well-illustrated technical press, architecture became international. The final section is, therefore, no longer only the story of a British development but includes drawings by international figures whose influence was world-wide: Wright, Behrens and Mies van der Rohe.

In spite of this revolution in design and building, and in spite of Internationalism, the twentieth century has already, like any other period of history, seen a succession of different styles, each with their national characteristics.

The International Style which started in 1911 with Gropius's work, was partly checked by Mendelsohn's Expressionism in the early 1920s and re-emerged in the late 1920s with Le Corbusier's houses in France and the work of Gropius, Mies and others at the Weissenhof housing scheme at Stuttgart in 1927. Apart from Behrens's house 'New Ways' at Northampton and Emberton's Olympia in London the style was slow to develop in England which until the early 1920s and 30s was dominated by Lutyens's scholarly classicism, by a Neo-Georgian style which looked to Tengbom and Ostberg in Sweden, and by the stripped-Classic monumentality which was close to the work of the American firm Corbett, Harrison & Associates shown here. After the Second World War Le Corbusier and Mies were the two principal influences – although increasingly from the late 1950s architects expressed a distaste for the Miesian doctrine 'less is more'. For example in 1959 the American architect Paul Rudolph presented the view: 'All problems can never be solved...Indeed it is characteristic of the twentieth century that architects are highly selective in determing which problems they want to solve. Mies for instance, makes wonderful buildings only because he ignores many aspects of a building. If he solved more problems, his buildings would be far less potent.'

A similar distaste for the 'banality' of modern architecture in 1964 led to James Stirling's design for the History Building at Cambridge, where he refused to compress the accommodation of the building into simple forms and where he intended the different elements to be clearly read and identified. This approach led to an architecture that became freer in its forms, but also in the 1970s to the era of revivals. The Modern Movement was thought to be at an end: instead architects incorporated historicist and picturesque elements into their work; housing became smaller in scale and brick respectable. The 'Post Modernism' of the mid 1970s looked to different figures and periods in the past – to Schinkel, Boullée, Ledoux and Neo-Classicism and to Lutyens and the Arts and Crafts Movement. But this is also paralleled in Britain by a 'high-tech' style, best seen in the work of the English architects Richard Rogers and Norman Foster.

In their draughtsmanship and presentation the architectural drawings of the Modern Movement also represent a break with the past. They are finely ruled, usually in black ink on tracing paper, without shadows or rendering; colour is rarely used. Mechanical aids lead to standardisation, in sheet sizes and particularly in lettering. The axonometric drawing generally supersedes the perspective; it is considered by architects to be a more honest form of representation.

Since the 1970s there has been a revival of interest in historical architectural drawings and present-day drawings have come to assume a new status. They are often coloured and elaborately rendered and many imitate the techniques of the past.

72 Frank Lloyd Wright (1867-1959)
Design for the Yahara Boat Club, Madison,
Wisconsin, 1902
Perspective
Sepia pen, with Wright's initials in a red square
(6¾ × 22) (170 × 560)
Provenance: Henry-Russell Hitchcock, by whom
the drawing was presented to the RIBA in 1965

The influence of Wright's architecture on the
international scene has been immense. This has
been due as much to what he said and wrote,
and to the mass of published material on his
architecture. One of the first books to publicize
his work was a collection of his designs published
by Ernest Wasmuth in 1910, *Ausgefahrte Bauten
und Entwurfe von Frank Lloyd Wright*. This project
was one of the schemes selected by Wasmuth
and although unexecuted, reached a wide
audience and had considerable influence on
modern architecture in Europe, notably on
Walter Gropius's and Adolf Meyer's Werkbund
Pavilion, Cologne, 1914, and on the Dutch De
Stijl movement, as can be seen in Robert Van
T'Hoff's villa at Huis ter Heide of 1916. It is a
remarkable design for 1902, preceding the
horizontality of the Robie House, Chicago, 1909,
and one of the first to use a reinforced concrete
flat-slab structure and to abandon the low-
pitched hip or gable roofs of his early Oak Park,
Chicago, houses.
   There is still doubt as to the draughtsman of
this drawing. It has been attributed by H. Allen
Brooks to Marion Mahony (1871-1962), one of
Wright's leading assistants from the 1890s,
because of a similarity to her known works in the
silhouette of the trees, leaves and method of
shading under the eaves. Mr Brooks admits,

however, that Barry Byrne, who was in the
Wright office, does not think the drawing is by
Mahony. Added to that the design is signed with
Wright's initials in a red square, which does not
appear in the Wasmuth reproduction. It is
therefore, possible that the drawing was a joint
effort, partly drawn by Mahony, signed by
Wright, and re-worked and traced by Wright or
an assistant when he was preparing the drawings
for publication in Fiesole in 1909. This would
certainly, in any case, have been the preparatory
drawing, not the actual drawing used for
publication, as all Wright's more subtle or
watercolour designs had to be redrawn in black
ink.

Lit: H. Allen Brooks, 'Frank Lloyd Wright and
the Wasmuth Drawings', *Art Bulletin*, XLVIII,
1966, pp. 193-201

73 Sir Edwin Lutyens (1869-1944)
Preliminary design for the Viceroy's House, New
Delhi, India, *c.* 1912-1913
Elevation & perspective of the east front
Pencil, pen & crayon on squared graph paper
(17 × 21½) (445 × 570)
Provenance: presented by Robert Lutyens,
(Lutyens's son) in 1951

The transfer of the seat of government of British
India from Calcutta to Delhi was proclaimed by
George V at the Delhi Coronation Durbar in
1911. Lutyens was invited to join the Delhi
Planning Commission in January 1912 and set
sail for India to choose the site for the new
capital on 1st April 1912. The site ultimately
chosen was Raisina Hill, and between the end of
April and early in the following year, when he
was officially appointed architect to the Viceroy's
House, he worked out rough plans and elevations
for the building which were revised and finalized
during the winter of 1913-1914. New Delhi was
inaugurated in February, 1931.

   In the autumn of 1912 a controversy raged in
the pages of *The Times* of London as to the
question of the proposed architectural style of
the new capital. Lutyens advocated the use of the
Western Classical traditions incorporating Indian
elements – but stopped short at the absurdity of
employing the Mogul pointed arch by arguing
that 'one cannot tinker with the round arch. God
did not make the Eastern rainbow pointed to
show his wide sympathies.' His design for the
Viceroy's House was a synthesis of abstract
European Classical and Indian architecture and
well expressed the synthesis aspired to by British
policy in India at the time.

   This sketch shows how the design evolved. The
principal Indian motifs have already been
incorporated: they are the chujja, the thin
projecting stone cornice which formed the
unifying horizontal line on the elevations, and
the chattri, the small Indian roof pavilion. In the
final design, however, the dome became squatter
and less Renaissance in character; it was based
on the smooth dome of the Great Stupa of
Sanchi.

   Lutyens made all his early preparatory designs
on squared sheets of a graph pad; he worked
rapidly, constantly evolving and jettisoning ideas
with 'hard labour' and 'hard thinking'. This is
one of 74 similar early studies for the Viceroy's
House at the RIBA.

Lit: C. Hussey, *The Life of Sir Edwin Lutyens*,
London, 1950, *passim*; M. Richardson, *Edwin
Lutyens, Catalogue of the Drawings Collection of the
Royal Institute of British Architects*, Farnborough,
1973, [58], pp. 17-18; G. Stamp, 'New Delhi' in
Lutyens, Arts Council catalogue of an exhibition,
London, 1981, pp. 33-42; R.G. Irving, *Indian
Summer, The Making of New Delhi*, London, 1981
passim.

74 Peter Behrens (1868-1940)
Preliminary design for New Ways, 508
Wellingborough Road, Northampton for W.J.
Bassett-Lowke, *c.* 1925
Perspective of the garden front
Pen & charcoal on tracing paper (15 × 23¼)
(380 × 590)
Provenance: presented by Mrs Bassett-Lowke in
1956

New Ways is a remarkable house by any
standards. It was the first consciously Modern
house in England and its design was shared, in
effect, by three people. Peter Behrens, then
Professor of Architecture at the Vienna Academy
of Fine Arts with an office in Berlin, designed the
elevations, the lounge, hall, and dining room.
The client prepared the plans, designed the
heating system and those rooms not dealt with
by Behrens but excluding the study which was

copied from designs made by Charles Rennie
Mackintosh (1868-1928) for a house he had
designed for Bassett-Lowke several years before.

The garden front shown here, was slightly
modified in execution so that the 'hood-moulds'
to the windows flanking the recessed centre were
omitted and the mouldings to the top of the
centre window were modified to a dentil-like
form. The house was constructed of rendered
brickwork painted white, the concrete cresting to
the parapet wall was painted black. These finials
were an Expressionist motif as was the V-plan
window bisecting the street elevation and some
of the details of Behrens's interior decoration.

The house still exists.

Lit: *Architectural Review*, LIX, 1926, pp.175-9

75 Sir Giles Gilbert Scott (1880-1960) with James
Theodore Halliday (1882-1932)
Design for Battersea Power Station, London
c. 1931
Perspective from the north bank of the Thames,
drawn by A.C. Webb (*c.* 1931-*c.* 1945)
Pencil & watercolour (23¼ × 17¾) (590 × 445)
Provenance: presented by Richard Gilbert Scott
(architect son of Sir Giles Gilbert Scott), in 1974

A.C. Webb's perspective shows the power station
as it was in 1934, when the first half had been
built and with two of its four chimneys.

More than any other building of the 1930s,
Battersea Power Station was probably the one
most associated in the public's mind with the
idea of modernity. But essentially Scott's work of
this period followed the middle way, neither
leaning towards traditionalism nor toward
modernism. He had taken notice though of the
early modernism of Dudok, Stockholm Town
Hall, North German Expressionist brick
architecture and some American architecture
and this influenced his work as much as his
strongly Gothic Revival background.

During the 1930s Giles Scott did a great deal of
consultancy work 'tidying up' other architect's
designs for large buildings. It was in this way,
apparently, that he became involved with the
design of Battersea Power Station, of which he
was the consultant for the exterior architecture
only. Engineering design began in 1927,
construction in 1929, architect J.T. Halliday
(1882-1932) of Halliday & Agate was then
brought in and in 1930 Scott was asked to
'improve' upon Halliday's proposals. The
'upturned table' form of the power station had
been established early on and though Scott could
not get the square-section chimneys that he
wanted, the fluted columns sensitively related to
the gigantic mass of the main structure and the
modelling of the huge elevations together with
the excellence of the brickwork are owed to him.

For the moment it remains as Pevsner
described 'one of the first examples in England
of frankly contemporary industrial architecture'
but the power station is due to be closed down
some time in 1983 and though listed by the
Government as being of architectural and
historical important the future for this London
landmark is uncertain.

G. Stamp, 'Sir Giles Gilbert Scott, The Problem of
Modernism' *Architectural Design*, XLIX,1979, pp.
72-83; G. Fisher, G. Stamp and others, *The Scott
Family, Catalogue of the Drawings Collection of the
Royal Institute of British Architects*, Amersham, 1981,
p.178

see Plate XV

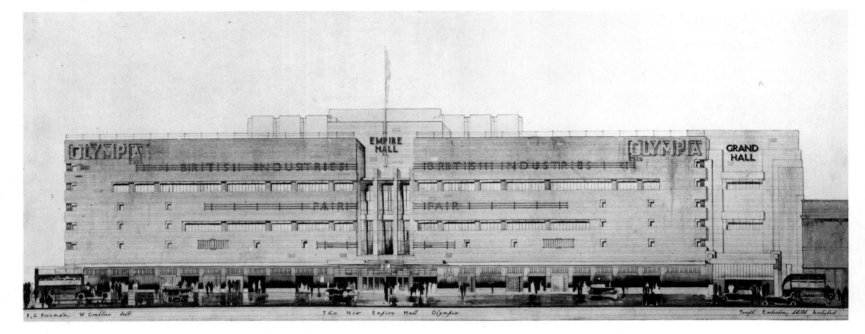

76 Joseph Emberton (1889-1956)
Design for the New Empire Hall, Olympia,
Hammersmith, London, 1929
Perspective of the main front, drawn by P.G.
Freeman (born 1907) and W. Crabtree (born
1905)
Pencil & watercolour (24 × 51¼) (610 × 1300)
Provenance: presented by H.M. Tardrew of
Emberton, Tardrew & Partners in 1966

Emberton was among the pioneers of modern
architecture in Britain. The Royal Corinthian
Yacht Club, Burnham-on-Crouch (1931),
Simpson's store, Piccadilly, London (1936), and
the HMV shop, Oxford Street, London (1938)
followed his first important commission, the
New Empire Hall, Olympia, 1929.

Sited next to the original exhibition hall
built in 1884, Emberton's Empire Hall was the
first multi-storeyed exhibition building
constructed in Britain. It was planned on a grid
of 50 foot squares, steel-framed with concrete
floors and brick-faced walls of which the main
front was rendered and painted white. The
design, as built, differs slightly from the
perspective shown here, the top right-hand
corner having stepped brick detail in the manner
of Berlage instead of the windows that were
retained for the opposite corner. Stylistically, the
building owes more to a later generation of
Dutch architects led by J.J.P. Oud and Mart Stam
whose belief in functionalism was shared by
Emberton. Every feature of the elevations in his

building, expresses an internal function and
inside, vent pipes, ducts and conduits run,
unconcealed, across the ceilings. Emberton's use
of artificial, daylight and display lighting was
advanced for that time and his use of lettering
well-judged. He went on to build another
exhibition hall at Olympia during the 1930s as
well as restaurants and a 1200-car garage
(thought to be the largest in Europe when built).
Olympia still stands and is still used for trade
fairs.

Lit: *Building*, V, 1930, pp.70-6; R. Ind, *Joseph
Emberton*, typescript of a book to be published by
Scolar Press, London, 1983

77 Corbett, Harrison and MacMurray, Hood and
Fouilhoux, and C. Howard Crane (Harvey Wiley
Corbett, 1873-1954, Wallace Kirkman Harrison,
born 1895 and William MacMurray, 1868-1941,
Raymond Hood, 1881-1934 and Jacques Andre
Fouilhoux, 1879-1945, and C. Howard Crane *c.*
1885-1952)
Alternative design for an International Music
Hall and Opera House, Hyde Park Corner,
London, *c.* 1933
Perspective
Pencil, black crayon & chinese white on board
(22½ × 28½) (570 × 725)
Provenance: purchased from a London
bookshop, in 1972

The project for an 'International Music Hall and
Opera House' by much the same team that
designed Radio City in New York (in London, C.
Howard Crane replaced Reinhard and
Hofmeister) was to be built on the site of St
George's Hospital, Hyde Park Corner. That
famous hospital was founded in 1719 and moved
to its present site in 1732 when Isaac Ware
converted Lanesborough House, a large private
mansion that stood among the fields of what was
then outer London. The hospital was rebuilt
1818-19 by William Wilkins in a Greek Revival
style and additions were made in 1859 and 1868.
From at least 1903, the hospital's Court of
Governors discussed proposals to rebuild the
hospital either on the same site or elsewhere in
London. These discussions intensified during the
1930s until World War II brought them to a halt.
In the 1970s a new St George's Hospital was built
at Tooting, South London and the old hospital
now stands empty.

It is not known where the initiative for a Radio
City in London came from but an obituary for
the theatrical entrepreneur Samuel L. Rothafel
(*New York Times*, 1.14.1936) noted that he visited
London and 'dickered with a proposal for the
erection of a mammoth motion picture theatre
with elaborate stage presentations. His plans did
not materialize however'. The architects offered
alternative treatments for the 6000-seat music hall.
Design A, shown here, was in an Imperialist style
that may have borrowed something of its heroic
decoration and scale from the Achilles

VIEW FROM WELLINGTON ΛRCH
DESIGN Λ

monument to the Duke of Wellington that is nearby; design B was in a Jazz Moderne style. The scheme is an interesting 'might have been', not least in the piquant contrast between the 20th century splendours of a Radio City and the exclusive environs of a royal park, Piccadilly and Belgravia that would have surrounded it.

Of the architects concerned in the project, two had already built in London. H.W. Corbett (Helmle & Corbett) designed Bush House, Aldwych (1925-32) in a Neo-Classical style of gigantic proportions, adorned by the two figures (16 feet high) of England and America holding a torch. Raymond Hood, with a British architect Gordon Jeeves, designed Ideal House near Oxford Circus (1928) using shiny, black granite cladding and multi-coloured Art Deco motifs.

Both of these distinctive contributions by American architects to the London scene are now protected by planning and historic building legislation.

Lit: C.H. Krinsky, *Rockefeller Center*, New York, 1978, pp. 164-87 *et passim*.

78 Ludwig Mies van der Rohe (1886-1969)
Design for the Library and Administration
Building of the Illinois Institute of Technology,
Chicago, Illinois, 1944
Perspective from the south-east
Pencil on board (32⅝ × 42½) (830 × 1080)
Provenance: presented by the architect in 1960.
Mies van der Rohe was awarded the RIBA Gold
Medal in 1959 and, as is customary, gave one of
his drawings to the Institute

In the summer of 1937, Mies van der Rohe left
Germany and went to live and work in the
United States. The following year he was made
Director of the School of Architecture at the
Illinois Institute of Technology (then the Armour
Institute). There followed, soon after, his first
important American commission – a plan for the
campus and the design of a number of its
buildings.
　　The Library and Administration Building was
one of the most significant of Mies's designs for
I.I.T. but it remained a project. Based on a 24-
foot modular grid that controlled the overall

design of the campus and its buildings, it would
have been, if built, 192 feet wide (24 feet × 8) and
312 feet long (24 × 13). Each of the three bays of
the south elevation, shown here, was stretched to
64 feet and the overall building height instead of
being in multiples of 12 feet was increased to 30
feet. In this way Mies achieved the impressive
proportions of the entrance front with its
transparent centre and flanking brick walls
contained within the structural steel skeleton of
the building. The Library, together with the
executed designs for I.I.T., established the
characteristics of Mies van der Rohe's work in
America: rectangular simplicity, subtle
proportions and perfect precision of details.

Lit: *Ludwig Mies van der Rohe, Drawings in the
Collection of the Museum of Modern Art*, introduction
and notes by L. Glaeser, New York, 1969, fig. 30.
The plans, elevations, sections, details and
further perspectives for this project are in the
Mies van der Rohe Collection, Museum of
Modern Art, New York.

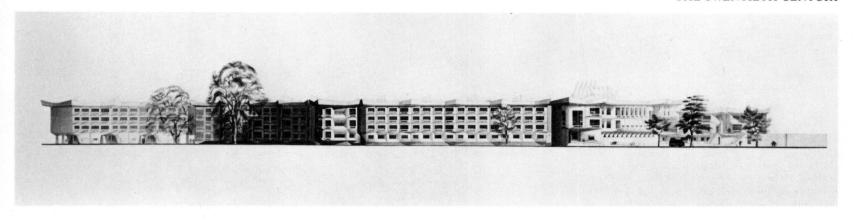

79 Howell, Killick, Patridge and Amis. (William Gough Howell, 1922-1974; John Killick, 1924-1972; John Partridge, born 1924; Stanley Amis, born 1924)
Competition design for Churchill College, Cambridge, 1959
South elevation
Pen, pencil & wash on paper, cut and pasted
(17½ × 60) (445 × 1520)
Provenance: presented by W.G. Howell in 1972

Howell, Killick, Partridge and Amis were among the four finalists in a two-stage limited competition for a new college at Cambridge named after Sir Winston Churchill (1874-1965). The competition was their first design for a major building (the partnership was set up in the same year) and though their scheme was unsuccessful, the planning based on pedestrian movement and the 'erupted skin-wall' were ideas that were to be taken up in their future work and in particular for St Anne's College, Oxford (1960-5).

HKPA belong to that first generation of post-war architects whose roots are firmly embedded in the Modern Movement, in the sense of that Movement's concern with principles and not outward appearances. The principle adhered to most strongly is 'the programme as a generator of form' and in a programme consisting of differing elements, those differences are expressed by separation and articulation rather than 'shoe-horning' into a single form.

For the Churchill College project where the brief included accommodation for students, Fellows and Master, dining halls and common rooms, library, offices and all the other requirements of collegiate life, HKPA devised a double-polygonal courtyard plan whose angularity was matched by that of the heavily modelled elevations. The intention behind the 'erupted skin' or 'slab chocolate bar' fronts with glass set behind the inner face of precast concrete splayed panels was to produce good natural lighting within. A pioneering aesthetic that was later taken up by other designers.

Drawn (as with so many competition drawings) by many hands, the cut and pasted technique was used as an aid to better photographic reproduction.

Lit: *Arena, the Architectural Association Journal,* LXXXII, 1966, pp. 95-122; *Howell Killick Partridge & Amis: Architecture,* introduction by S. Cantacuzino, London, 1981, p. 56 *et passim.*

80 James Stirling (born 1926)
Design for the University of Cambridge History
Faculty building, Sidgwick Avenue, Cambridge,
1964
Axonometric
Graphos pen & indian ink on tracing paper
(9⅞ × 8⅞) (250 × 195)
Provenance: lent by the architect, 1982

The competition for a new History building at
Cambridge was limited to Architects'
Co-Partnership, David Roberts and James
Stirling; Stirling's scheme was the successful one.
After the competition it was found that only half
the proposed site was available and Stirling's
design had to be re-located on this smaller site
and turned from its east-facing aspect to a
northerly one. Few changes were made to the
original project.

The brief included staff study rooms, seminar
rooms, common rooms, offices and a library
that, seating 300 readers and with 12,600 square
feet of shelving occupied about half the total
area. While the other competition entries
proposed two separate blocks, Stirling's offered a
totally integrated scheme and a library planned
to allow for the closest supervision. This last was
achieved by a radial layout of the two-storey
bookstack on a quarter circle plan that with the
reading room was overlooked by a control desk
raised four feet above the main floor. Such an
adaptation of a nineteenth century notion of
library planning, following a spate of book thefts
from other Cambridge libraries, commended
itself to librarians and academics. The key to the
close contact between the reading room and the
rest of the History Faculty accommodation lies in
the arrangement of windowed corridors as
galleries around the reading room so that library
and class room activities are unified.

Structurally, the History Building is made up
of three distinct but interdependent elements: a
seven-storey L-shaped block, a two-storey block
that connects the two ends of the L-block and is
cranked twice on plan to enclose the book stack,
and the glazed roof over the reading room.

The axonometric drawing made by Stirling of
his scheme was submitted with the competition
report to the competition committee. Like many
of his other drawings, it was later mounted and
framed in a standard museum manner.

Axonometric projections show to the client
'the space, the structure, geometry, function and
detail together without distortion' and for the
architect 'makes it possible to assess the total
architectural consequences of design decisions'.

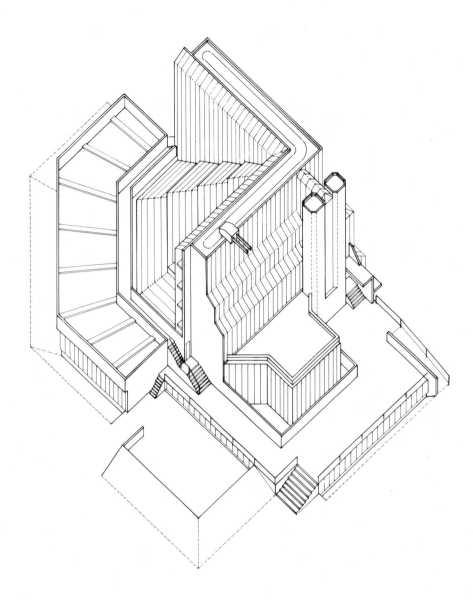

Lit: *Architectural Review*, CXLIV, 1968, pp. 329-38;
Architectural Design, XXXVIII, 1968, pp. 454-74;
P. Booth & N. Taylor, *Cambridge New Architecture*,
London, 1970, pp. 179-82; *James Stirling*,
catalogue of an exhibition, RIBA Drawings
Collection, London, 1974, *passim*.

81 Norman Robert Foster (born 1935)
Design for the Sainsbury Centre for the Visual
Arts, University of East Anglia, Norwich, Norfolk,
for Sir Robert and Lady Sainsbury and the
University of East Anglia, 1974-78
Isometric sections 1 and 2 and preparatory
sketches (only one illustrated).
Rotring pen on foil (33 × 45) (841 × 1138) each
Provenance: lent by the architect, 1983

The Sainsbury Centre was built to house the art
collection of Sir Robert and Lady Sainsbury and
also to provide accommodation for the
University's History of Art Department, an
exhibition area, senior common room, restaurant
and workshops. The original intention was that it
should be an art centre where works of art
should be enjoyed by scientist and art student
alike; an overhead bridge links the complex to
the existing pedestrian spine of the university
buildings designed by Sir Denys Lasdun. The
Centre takes the form of a Miesian hangar. Its
tubular steel structure is clad on its exterior with
silver grey, aluminium panels, and internally
with adjustable, perforated aluminium louvres
which temper the environmental conditions
within the building. The end walls are glazed. Its
'high-tech' aesthetic hinges on the language of
the modern, material world of finely detailed,
industrial finishes.

Lit: *Architectural Review*, CLXIV, 1978, pp. 345-
362; *Architectural Design*, XLIX, 1979, pp. 1-32

82 Richard Rogers (born 1933)
Design for the rebuilding of Lloyds, Leadenhall
Street, City of London, 1981
Elevation to Leadenhall Street, drawn to a metric
scale of 1:100
Pen, airbrush & coloured felt-tip pen on 'en tout
cas' paper (43 × 61) (1090 × 1550)
Provenance: lent by the architect, 1982

The rebuilding of the headquarters of Lloyds,
the insurance underwriters, was the subject of a
limited international competition in 1977-8 won
by Richard Rogers + Partners. The scheme
provides a half-million square feet of highly
flexible space enclosing a 200 foot high glazed
atrium surrounded by six stainless steel-
clad satellites containing all the service and
access elements.

Lit: D. Cruickshank, 'Lloyds redevelopment, City
of London', *Architectural Review*, CLXIX, 1981,
pp. 277-82

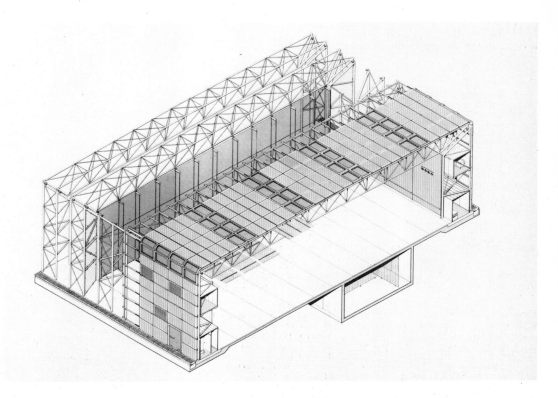

LLOYD'S REDEVELOPMENT
RICHARD ROGERS + PARTNERS   49 PRINCES PLACE HOLLAND PARK LONDON W11 4QA

LEADENHALL ST. ELEVATION
DRAWING NUMBER 970-007/3P · FEBRUARY 1981

Index

Roman numerals refer to the colour plates

Printed and bound by Dai Nippon
Printing Co. Ltd., Tokyo, Japan